HONEY

HONEY

ANGELO PROSPERI-PORTA

EVERYDAY
RECIPES FOR
COOKING
AND BAKING
with
NATURE'S
SWEETEST
SECRET
INGREDIENT

TouchWood
Editions

I DEDICATE THIS BOOK to those first few brave souls who gathered honey from hives in the wild, and to those who began and continue to work in what we know now as the honey industry. And to the honeybees themselves. Without these marvelous insects we would be missing not only a delicious and nutritious source of natural sugar but also approximately 30 to 35 percent of the fruits, nuts, and vegetables we consume. I don't want to imagine a scenario without the great diversity with which we are blessed.

CONTENTS

FOREWORD

Angelo Prosperi-Porta and I share a common passion–for upholding the traditions of our family kitchens and the gardens that supplied them. We love to share the harvest by creating wonderful meals for friends and family. This is, after all, what has defined us as humans down through the ages.

For Angelo, it was his parents who instilled in him a great appreciation for fine traditional Italian food and a humble respect for kitchen gardens. It was a family tradition he carried with him to Cooper's Cove Guesthouse, where I first met him, and where he would harvest edible flowers, herbs, vegetables, fruits, and berries from his own land. We both, it seems, appreciate the ritual so much that we don't mind the sore backs from weeding or the dirt under our fingernails.

We both also love to watch the honeybees that fly through our little patches of paradise, linking our gardens and pollinating the plants that produce the foods we enjoy so much.

Honey–used to enhance natural, wholesome, and delicious ingredients–is the focus of this cookbook. These are simple, straightforward recipes with a traditional flair. But this is much more than just a cookbook. *Honey* is about the time-honored ancient relationship between humans and honeybees.

We are currently experiencing a resurgence of appreciation for farm-fresh, locally grown, organic, natural, and whole unprocessed foods. These words have become the new mantras for those who seek the satisfaction of a meal cooked and prepared the way our ancestors would have enjoyed it. We have a better understanding of what *good food* is and what it takes to produce it ourselves, or at least what it takes for the producers at local farmers' markets to bring their bounty to the table.

The honeybee is the anchor for so much of the fresh, nutritious food we desire, and what we need now is a little insight into how important a role these insects play in maintaining a clean environment, healthy soils, and pure water.

Honey, therefore, is not just a collection of recipes by a master chef of international acclaim with decades of passion and generations of tradition behind him. It is an entreaty for a convergence of thought–for people to come together in understanding that such a book would not be possible without the existence of the hardworking honeybees. That without them, we would lose much more than just nature's sweetest secret ingredient.

Bob Liptrot
Master beekeeper
Tugwell Creek Meadery
(www.tugwellcreekfarm.com)
Vancouver Island, Canada

ACKNOWLEDGMENTS

My great appreciation goes to those who made this book a reality. The gang at Touchwood Editions: former publisher Ruth Linka, in particular, who helped set me on the path of writing about and creating with honey, and current associate publisher Taryn Boyd, for her enthusiasm and good humor, not to mention patience and understanding—life does get in the way sometimes! Cailey Cavallin contributed greatly in helping to make things make sense with her editing and suggestions. Thanks also to Pete Kohut for his layout of the book and to Grace Yaginuma for her proofreading and corrections.

Bob Liptrot from Tugwell Creek Farm has been an ongoing inspiration. We first met Bob and his partner, Dana LeCompte, almost two decades ago, when they came to visit us at Cooper's Cove Guesthouse, and it has been exciting to watch them develop the successful enterprise that they operate today. Bob's technical information and suggestions were very helpful.

Nadine Boyd and Gary Faessler did a wonderful job with the photography. Gary, thanks for being there at the last minute.

My best taste-tester and life partner Ina Haegemann has always kept me on track, with a few detours along the way. Her critiques and suggestions helped make many of the recipes even tastier, especially the desserts!

The plight of the honeybees that produce the product we love is in the news these days and has been for many years. It is important for us to realize that nothing happens without a cause. We are not sure exactly why bees and other pollinators around the world are suffering. Whether it is climate change, overuse of pesticides and insecticides, or other causes, we can all do our part by supporting sustainable sources of honey, limiting or eliminating our own use of chemicals, and doing what we can to contribute to a healthy environment for all. The bees have been the most important contributors to this book.

INTRODUCTION

THE BUSY WORLD OF BEES

There are many reasons to cook with honey or, at the very least, begin using it to replace some of the white sugar in your diet. Though honey is of course still a sugar, just in a different form, it is the healthier option—a natural whole food, it is rich in minerals and vitamins. And you need less of it to achieve the same level of sweetness. But the main reason I use honey is that there are so many varieties (each with its own distinct flavor) available to choose from and they just taste so good!

But before we get to the honey, we must start with the bees.

Honeybees are responsible for a large percentage of our crops, from the familiar fruits and vegetables we eat to the sweet clover and alfalfa farmers plant as feed for livestock. So, not only are bees important to the production of foods like apples and potatoes, they also indirectly play a part in some of the meats you may eat.

Though other insects, including wild native bees, and a few species of birds (for instance, the hummingbird) do contribute to pollination, it is the European honeybee, *Apis mellifera*, on which industrial agriculture greatly depends. These honeybees were introduced to North America by European colonizers around the year 1625. Until that point, North America did not know honey as we know it today.

The introduction of the honeybee and large-scale beekeeping also made it possible for farmers to expand their crops. Today, beehives are trucked across the continent—they travel according to the blooming seasons and provide the pollination needed to produce many fruit, vegetable, and nut crops.

One amazing example is California's Central Valley almond industry. One thousand square miles of the valley are covered with almond trees, which produce 80 percent of the world's crop. It takes approximately 1.5 million hives, up to 30 billion bees, to do the job. Before and after their work in the almond orchards, the hives are sent out on a regular rotation to pollinate everything from apples to zucchini.

Wild bees can and should be encouraged in our yards, gardens, and fields. Those who do not have the time or space for a garden can help bees and other pollinators simply by sowing a variety of native wildflowers wherever there is an open space, no matter how big or small. Other bee-friendly things you can do in your own backyard include no longer treating your lawn with chemicals or even replacing the grass with nectar-rich flowers, as pesticides and herbicides have shown to be detrimental to the health of bees and other pollinators. Since approximately 2004, honeybees have been disappearing, in a phenomenon known as colony collapse disorder (CCD). Seemingly healthy worker bees leave the hive to go about the business of foraging and collecting nectar and pollen, and never return, leaving the rest of the colony to die in the hive. A definitive cause has yet to be pinpointed, but there is evidence pointing to the overuse of these harmful substances. (Other suspected causes are Varroa mites, which suck moisture from the bee's body, and Nosema spores, which live in the bee's stomach, weakening them until they die. Other invasive species of mites and insects are also suspected, along with severe winters.)

By sowing a variety of wildflowers, we can help ensure the continued survival of pollinators like bees–and discover the practical results that a small effort can return, such as a healthy, vital, and productive garden. Wildflower seed mixes are easily available from most nurseries. If you're looking for something a little different, mixed herb plantings can make wonderful, less formal borders for your garden, while combinations of different varieties of sage–for example, green, purple, variegated, and pineapple–with their varied colors and bloom times, will attract bees for an extended season.

There are many plants that supply higher amounts of nectar for bees; they can be planted in a wide mixed distribution or arranged as preferred. Though by no means a definitive list, the following is a broad sample of these plants.

Alfalfa	Catnip	Honeysuckle	Rosemary
Alyssum	Clover	Lavender	Sage
Apple	Cornflower	Lemon balm	Snowberry
Aster	Cosmos	Marjoram	Sunflower
Basil	Cucumber	Mint	Thyme
Bee balm	Dandelion	Mustard	Wallflower
Bergamot	Echinacea	Oregano	
Borage	Goldenrod	Rape	
Calendula	Hollyhock	Red clover	

Chefs and cooks the world over pride themselves on producing great food with high-quality ingredients that they have either sourced themselves or had a hand in producing. The raising of bees for a personal supply of honey not only helps the general health of the gardens where they grow their ingredients (as well as other gardens in the area), but also delivers a product that can have its own unique characteristics for the cook to exploit. A growing trend over the last decade has been for homeowners and chefs alike to keep their own bees. Even hotels and restaurants have begun to bring in bees and beekeepers, placing beehives on rooftops and in other available spaces. A well-known North American hotel chain has had beehives for several years on many of its properties in Canada, the United States, and other countries, which has allowed them to add new, unique creations to their menus. This rooftop setup is also being enhanced by the installation of containers for herb plants, fruit trees, berry bushes, and more, wherever space allows. Many of these sites are in the middle of large cities and are thriving.

My own attempt to raise bees, though both educational and fun, was short lived. This was not due to failure on either my part or the part of the bees but rather to overwhelming success. In the early spring of 2007, with the help of my friend Bob Liptrot, beekeeper and mead maker at Tugwell Creek, I obtained a hive and its contents from an amateur beekeeper who could no longer keep the bees. With some guidance from Bob and information I found on beekeeping websites, I built extra boxes, called supers, and we set up the hive in a sunny south-facing location in the center of my garden, behind the bed and breakfast my wife and I used to run. My motivation for keeping bees was a simple one. I had planted several fruit trees in my garden as I have always enjoyed growing my own produce. The bees helped ensure adequate pollination for the trees; the honey they produced was a wonderful byproduct of this process.

Bees need a certain amount of space to go about the business of raising a brood (future bees), collecting and processing nectar into honey, and storing the honey. Each healthy hive contains a queen bee, several hundred male drones, and up to 20,000 female worker bees. The role of the drones is to mate with the queen to produce the brood. Once they have done so, their job is done. The queen bee then lays thousands of eggs. She fertilizes some, which will hatch and grow to become (female) worker bees; the rest of the eggs remain unfertilized and become (male) drones. (Young worker bees raise this next generation.)

The job of the worker bees is to gather nectar and pollen to supply the hive with food. These gatherers travel up to five miles each trip. Working at the rate they do, being constantly on the go, the lifespan of a worker bee during the productive season is only about six weeks. They literally work themselves to death.

Their primary target is nectar, which, in most cases, is drawn up from the base of flower blossoms. The nectar is then stored in the bees' honey sacs, where enzymes are introduced until enough nectar has been collected to allow the bees to return to the hive. In the act of collecting the nectar, the bees' legs, which are covered in very fine, statically charged hairs, gather the pollen from the anthers of the flower and deposit a small amount on the stigma, initiating the pollination of the seed. Pollen is very high in protein and is collected as food for the brood.

Once the gatherers return to the hive, the nectar is passed on to other worker bees and processed further—the bees in the hive repeatedly pump the nectar in and out of themselves, until it reaches a carbohydrate content level of approximately 55 percent. The nectar is then deposited into the honeycomb. Here the nectar goes through a process called ripening. The enzymes introduced when the nectar was inside of the bees act to convert disaccharide sucrose into fructose and glucose. In addition, the water content of the nectar is reduced to between 14 and 18 percent, low enough to prevent the growth of bacteria, which would spoil the honey. This is accomplished by the worker bees—they fan the interior of the hive to remove moisture. This fanning process is also used to keep air circulating in the hive, cooling or heating as needed. Once the honey is sufficiently concentrated, or ripe, the honeycomb is capped and sealed with a layer of wax. This will be the food that sustains the hive over the winter or in times when it is not possible to collect nectar. The pollen the bees collect is stored in a separate area of the hive.

Over the centuries bees have evolved (through their interactions with beekeepers and scientists) to produce much more honey than they would normally need over a season and to sustain the hive through the fall and winter. For this reason, we can harvest the honey and continue to maintain the health of the hive.

When a colony is successful to the point where space becomes an issue, the natural outcome is for the hive to expand. This process is called swarming. A larva is selected to be the hive's new queen and is fed royal jelly throughout its larval stage and adult life. (Royal jelly is a secretion which when fed to the larva triggers its development into a queen, with all of her egg-laying capabilities.) When the new queen reaches maturity, the "surplus queen" (i.e., the old queen) departs the hive in search of a new site. A swarm of up to 30,000 bees, which are programmed to follow her, will go too.

In my case, the queen chose a small ornamental tree next to the entrance of one of our guestrooms. Not an ideal spot with guests arriving for the weekend. The bees were gathered and encouraged back into the original hive.

About a month later, the swarm once again departed the hive and this time gathered in a hedge on the edge of my property, which happens to be beside a busy road and a bus stop. Picture two men (myself and my friend Bob), covered head to toe in white bee suits, on a ladder next to the busy road trying to encourage 30,000 bees into a cardboard box just as the school bus arrived. An interesting sight for the school kids, I'm sure, but a potentially dangerous situation with a cloud of bees hanging over the road.

Since this second swarm, I have unfortunately had to abandon my quest to harvest my own honey until I have a more suitable location. The experience was a fascinating one, though, and I learned a lot in regards to the social life of bees and the fact that if given the right conditions, they can and will flourish. I look forward to my next attempt and in the meantime will take great pleasure in using this delicious natural product we call honey.

HONEY VARIETIES

lthough the following list does not include every variety of honey available to consumers in North America, it is a good representation. Many of these varieties will be familiar to you while others may seem a little "exotic."

The unique flavors and characteristics of different honeys are determined by many factors, including environment (mineral content of the soil, weather, etc.), available blossoms, locality, and the age of the honey. There are over 200 recognized substances in honey that contribute in some way to its color, flavor, and nutritional value.

When buying honey, a simple though imperfect rule to keep in mind is light-colored honeys are usually milder while darker honeys are stronger in flavor.

HONEY TYPES	REGION	CHARACTERISTICS	BEST USES
Acacia	Europe, North America	Very clear and pure in appearance. Delicate floral flavor. Remains liquid longer due to high fructose content.	Sweetens beverages without altering their flavor. Great with salty cheeses.
Alfalfa	Canada, USA	Subtle spice flavor. Mild floral spice aroma.	Great for baked goods.
Blackberry	North America	Dark in color. Floral aroma. A little more acidic than other varieties.	Great as a condiment for savory appetizers and with sweet bites.
Blueberry	Eastern North America	Mild, pleasant blueberry flavor, with a slight tang.	Good in fruit-based desserts and herbal teas.
Buckwheat	North America	Dark in color. Not as sweet as other varieties, with a slightly bitter but not unpleasant finish. Contains more iron and antioxidants than milder honeys.	Great in savory dishes.

HONEY TYPES	REGION	CHARACTERISTICS	BEST USES
Chestnut	Italy/Western Europe	Dark in color. Not as sweet as other varieties, with a slightly bitter but not unpleasant finish.	Great in savory dishes or anywhere a full flavor is desired.
Clover	Canada, USA	Color can be anywhere from clear white to light amber to amber. Very popular and widely available. Mild and sweet but rounded flavor.	Good in sauces, dressings, and baking.
Coffee Blossom	Mexico, Hawaii, South America, and many other coffee-producing countries	Amber to dark in color. Rich flavor, with hints of citrus, licorice, and brown sugar.	Good in meat glazes or with an aged cheese plate.
Fireweed	North America	Light in color, with a delicate buttery flavor.	Great for baking, glazing, barbecuing, and smoking fish and meat.
Honeydew, or Forest Honey	Europe, North America	Dark to very dark in color. Medium sweetness and intensity of flavor. Woody taste. Varies greatly from source to source.	Good for many different applications due to its varied characteristics.
Lavender	France	Sweet floral aroma. Rich flavor. Slightly acidic taste.	Good in baking and desserts.
Linden	Eastern North America, Europe, Asia	Light to amber in color. Woody aroma. Described as mildly medicinal, due to hints of balsam, mint, and menthol. Low acidity. Medium sweetness, with a slightly bitter finish.	Good for desserts, sorbets, and sherbets, as well as in herbal teas.
Manuka	New Zealand, Australia	Medium to dark in color. Strong floral bouquet. Prized for its antibiotic and medicinal properties when sold as "medicinal grade." Comes from the blossoms of the manuka or tea tree.	Good in savory dishes, baking, and desserts where a strong flavor is desired.
Miele di Melata, or Miele di Bosco	Italy	A honeydew honey produced from the honeydew of apple trees or forest trees. Thick in consistency. Delicate aroma. Slight apple finish.	Good on fruit-based desserts.
Orange Blossom	USA, Australia, Spain	Light to amber in color, with a pleasant floral bouquet and a light citrus finish. Extra sweet finish.	Great for desserts, syrups, dessert sauces, and baking.
Wildflower	North America	Often referred to as mixed floral. Can be light and mild to dark and rich.	Versatile and good for most applications.

What is honeydew? Honeydew honey, or forest honey, is not produced from nectar but rather from a sticky substance excreted by plant-sucking insects like aphids. The insects break through the tender areas of coniferous and deciduous trees and ingest the sap, which is very low in the protein the insects are after and very high, relatively, in sugars. After digesting the proteins, the insects excrete the remaining sap onto leaves and branches and even the ground. This sweet substance is sought after by many other insects, including bees. In the case of honeybees, it is processed into honey, often mixed with the nectar of blossoms, though in some instances it is the main ingredient in the actual honey produced. Honeydew honey tends to have a stronger taste, more mineral in flavor and less sweet.

Honeymoon is a term that dates back to the 1500s. It comes from the Old English *hony moone*. Hony, or honey, refers to the newfound and sweet marital bliss felt by a newly married couple, while moone, or moon, refers to how long the marital bliss would last (i.e., one lunar cycle). Sounds like a great start, doesn't it? In modern times, the term refers mostly to the sweet beginnings of continued marital bliss.

It also has roots that go back to the 5th century, when newly married couples would consume mead, the fermented alcoholic honey drink, for the first month or moon of their marriage. Mead was reputed to be an aphrodisiac. Now that's a good start!

NONCULINARY/
MEDICINAL USES

As you go through this book, you'll discover how wonderfully diverse honey can be—and how delicious it can taste in a wide variety of recipes. But did you know that honey also has nonculinary uses? Here are some of the ways you can use honey outside of the kitchen:

- Eat raw local honey to help reduce allergy symptoms.
- Apply honey to dry skin to rehydrate.
- Apply honey to wounds and small, nonserious burns to help them heal. (All honey has some level of hydrogen peroxide; this is what gives it many of its antibacterial properties and makes it as effective as some antibiotic ointments.)
- Use manuka honey—it is said to be the best medicinal honey for treating burns, infections, and gastrointestinal problems.
- Take a teaspoon of honey as a cough suppressant.
- Use honey as a skin cleanser and face mask.
- Combine honey and apple cider vinegar for a great hair conditioner that will add body and luster to you hair.
- Drink a cup of warm milk mixed with a big spoonful of honey to help with insomnia.

As I've noted, honey is a natural cough suppressant; it is also a soother for sore throats, as you'll discover with the wonderful lozenge recipe on page 12. The lozenges are one example of honey as a natural remedy, but these little candies are good any time. Another great example is this hot ginger drink to help you fight colds.

HOT GINGER COLD REMEDY

It seems that no matter which professional kitchen I find myself in, if it's winter and someone has a cold, a version of this drink is quickly thrown together to help soothe the symptoms. The kicker ingredient is the cayenne pepper. Cayenne stimulates blood flow to peripheral areas of the body, warming you up. It is sweat inducing and helps to relieve congestion and reduce fever. Ginger is known to relieve upset stomach and feelings of nausea and also induces blood flow. And lemon juice provides a boost of vitamin C, while honey also helps to calm the stomach. The proportions listed here can be adjusted to strengthen the drink, or cut for something a little milder.

SERVES 1

3–4 thin slices peeled ginger

Juice of ½ large lemon

2 Tbsp honey

1–2 pinches of cayenne pepper

On a cutting board, crush the ginger slices using the back of a large knife. Place the ginger in the bottom of a large coffee mug. Add the rest of the ingredients and fill the mug with boiling water.

Stir to combine and dissolve the honey. Steep for 3 to 4 minutes and drink hot.

HONEY-LEMON
THROAT SOOTHER

Candy making is simple but relies on accuracy. Think of this recipe in 4 steps: make the infusion; combine the infusion with the honey and cook; add the essential oils and allow the mixture to cool; and finally, shape, cut, and wrap the finished product. A little patience is required when cooking the honey syrup, so set aside at least 1 hour to complete the recipe. You will be tempted to increase the heat as you wait for the desired temperature, but don't do it. Honey burns easily once the moisture evaporates and the temperature increases.

A few special pieces of equipment will also help ensure success. You will need a 2-quart high-sided, heavy-bottomed saucepan, a candy thermometer or heatproof thermometer that reads up to at least 300°F, silicone or parchment paper, and sterile rubber gloves to handle and shape the hot mixture once cooked.

MAKES 40 LOZENGES

1½ cups cold water

1 cup tightly packed fresh rosemary leaves, coarsely chopped

5 fresh or dried bay leaves, crushed

⅓ cup fennel seeds, crushed with the back of a heavy knife

Grated zest of 1 organic lemon

1½ cups honey

1 Tbsp lemon oil (see Chef's Tip)

2 tsp eucalyptus oil (see Chef's Tip)

Pour the water into a 2-quart saucepan and add the rosemary, bay leaves, and fennel seeds. Bring to a boil on high heat and cook for 2 minutes.

Remove from heat and stir in the lemon zest. Set aside for 20 minutes.

Strain the mixture through a cheesecloth (a coffee filter will substitute nicely) and return to a clean pan.

Stir in the honey, return to the stove, and bring to a boil. Reduce heat to medium.

The temperature will rise quickly to around 220°F and then will take up to 20 minutes to reach the desired 300°F.

Stir frequently to prevent overflow and scorching. As the honey cooks, it will foam up more. Adjust heat accordingly.

Place a sheet of parchment paper on a heat-resistant surface and have the oils and a pair of rubber gloves ready.

Once the honey mixture has reached 300°F, remove from heat immediately and stir to cool for a couple of minutes. Add the lemon and eucalyptus oils and stir to combine, continuing to stir to allow the mixture to cool evenly.

Once the mixture begins to thicken, pour it onto the parchment paper in a long line. Put on the gloves and begin to work the candy into a rope approximately 16 to 18 inches long by lifting the edge of the paper and folding the mixture over. Divide into 2 ropes.

One at a time, roll the ropes into 16-inch lengths that are about ¾ inch thick. As the ropes cool, alternately roll the ropes to keep them round, or let them flatten slightly.

Once hardened but still pliable (this will happen quickly depending on the temperature of the work surface), cut each of the ropes into 20 individual pieces using a pair of heavy kitchen shears or a knife. Allow to cool completely.

To store, individually wrap each piece of candy in a square of parchment paper, or place in layers divided by parchment paper in an airtight container. These will keep indefinitely.

CHEF'S TIP
Food-grade essential oils can be purchased at health food stores and specialty shops.

WHY COOK WITH HONEY?

Honey contributes greatly to the quality of baked goods. It is hygroscopic, meaning it attracts moisture. This helps keep baked items moist, even absorbing moisture in humid conditions and giving baked goods a longer shelf life. It also contributes to the chewiness and texture of baked goods. Sugar contributes sweetness of course, but honey contributes sweetness along with flavor and a more attractive browning to items such as yeast breads, quick breads, and muffins.

It is also a natural preservative so it is an ideal sweetener for poaching fruit and making preserves. A unique method of preservation in this book is my use of honey along with Canadian whisky to preserve salmon (see recipe on page 64).

Honey is more expensive than sugar but not as much as one would think. Due to its higher levels of fructose, honey is sweeter than sugar; therefore, less is needed to achieve the same level of sweetness. One cup of honey is equal to 1¼ cups of sugar plus ¼ cup of water.

This should be of interest to those who monitor their caloric and carbohydrate intake, because while 1 tablespoon of honey contains 64 calories and about 17 grams of carbohydrates, and the equivalent amount of sugar has about 46 calories and about 12.6 grams of carbs, less honey is needed to sweeten your food.

There are also health benefits to eating honey. Due to the methods used in processing white sugar–high heat to boil down raw sugar juice, for example–any vitamins and enzymes naturally occurring in the sugar are destroyed. Honey on the other hand is only minimally heated during the extraction process, never reaching more than 110°F (43°C). So raw honey retains not only its vitamins and enzymes, but also its naturally occurring antioxidant and antimicrobial properties.

(There is minor risk to eating raw–unpasteurized–honey, but only to infants under the age of one year. Infant botulism can occur when an infant ingests *Clostridium botulinum*, which can be present in soil, dust, and honey. When ingested this can produce spores that multiply in the immature digestive tract of infants. But this is a very rare and treatable occurrence.)

Although present in small amounts, the vitamins and enzymes in honey, as well as its antioxidant and antimicrobial properties, all contribute to a healthy diet. Unfortunately many of the benefits that come from using raw honey in your diet are lost when the honey is heated. The enzymes and antioxidant properties are only maintained as long as the honey is not heated above 140°F (60°C). And the antimicrobial properties of honey are most prevalent in raw honey. However, the improvements in flavor, texture, and consistency are maintained even through the cooking process.

And that's the most important reason why I cook with honey–it tastes great and adds a little something extra to dishes and baked goods of all kinds.

ABOUT THE RECIPES

When I want to create a new recipe, the process begins like this: I have an idea. I see some ingredients in a market or growing together in my garden. These ingredients were there yesterday, in the same spot, but they didn't inspire. Don't ask me why. Today, however, inspiration strikes and my mind immediately goes to what tasty dish I can create.

I usually keep things simple. I want a few key ingredients with characteristics and flavors that blend well together and yet standout individually in the finished dish. In the past, I have written about relying on characteristics—the basic tastes of sweet, sour, salty, and bitter—as much as on individual flavors.

The recipes in this book were specifically created to show the ease of incorporating *honey* into your everyday cooking. Your first thought when you hear this may be "I don't want all my cooking to be sweet!" But a little sweetness in every dish is actually a good thing, because a successful dish is one that is balanced.

By that I mean the flavors of the dish should come together in a way that lets the eater taste all of the contributing ingredients. Though the goal, of course, is always to have the main item, whether it is meat, or fish, or a vegetable, come through, a well-balanced dish will not be dominated by any one ingredient. Instead, it will have an equal balance of sweet, savory, and salty. These characteristics work in unison on the taste buds to bring out the flavors in food.

A good example is my Beef Tenderloin with Gorgonzola Cheese and Honey Pepper Streusel (page 100). With a rich beef cut, I like a full-bodied red wine. But red wines contain tannins; they are what give you that astringent feeling in your mouth. To balance the dish, these tannins need to be "softened." This is where the honey comes in. Honey, in this case a dark, full-flavored buckwheat variety, helps cut the astringency and rounds out the flavors. The same sort of balancing act happens with the Gorgonzola cheese and the honey pepper streusel, to finish the dish. Gorgonzola is a very rich, spicy (and delicious!) blue-veined cow's milk cheese from Italy. Here, the honey in the streusel helps cut the richness of the cheese.

Balance of flavor is not the only contribution made by honey, though. Honey also helps in the browning of certain foods such as baked goods and roasted or grilled meats and vegetables. Grilled or roasted fruits also benefit from honey. As well it adds viscosity to sweet and savory sauces, allowing the elimination or reduction of the amount of extra thickener (usually a starch) that is needed. And due to the wide variety of honeys available, each with distinct flavor and color, one can experiment when using honey, whereas that just does not happen with most other sweeteners.

Although I have included some historical and health information throughout the book, I certainly do not claim any authority on the subject of bees and honey. My goal is simply to lead the way to different avenues for using honey to enhance your cooking repertoire.

With practice, you will learn to look at ingredients in your mind's eye and see how to combine them to create something delicious. Improvisation in the kitchen can lead to wonderful things. If a recipe calls for red wine but all you have is a rosé or a white, is your dish going to be a disaster? Of course not. If you need Gorgonzola and you only have a delicious blue brie, lucky you! Give yourself the freedom to play. Food is for sustenance, but it is also to be enjoyed. Get in that kitchen and have fun!

Mead, by definition, is any alcoholic beverage made by fermenting honey. This includes certain types of beers and wines. The honey provides carbohydrates that are converted into alcohol by either naturally occurring or introduced yeast.

THE CHALLENGES
OF SUBSTITUTING
HONEY FOR SUGAR

In some recipes it is very easy to substitute honey for sugar or other sweeteners. Consider most barbecue sauces or sweet glazes. They are usually reduced or boiled down to the desired consistency, so the replacement of the sweetener is not determined by an exact proportion but rather by your own taste buds.

Baking, on the other hand, presents more of a challenge, as the consistency of baked goods is determined by a set formula. Often the proportions would be greatly affected if sugar was replaced one-for-one by honey, which is not only sweeter but also contains approximately 18 percent water. This wouldn't have much of an effect on, for example, a chocolate brownie square, but it would mean the difference in whether an almond sponge cake will hold its shape.

Another characteristic of honey to keep in mind is that it contributes greatly to the browning of cooked foods, especially baked goods. Using lower temperatures and/or cutting back the cooking time can control this.

Honey is composed of primarily carbohydrates (natural sugars) and water as well as trace enzymes, minerals, vitamins, and amino acids. It also contains flavonoids and phenolic acids, which act as antioxidants, scavenging and eliminating free radicals. In general, darker honeys have a higher antioxidant content than lighter honeys.

Another challenge presents itself when substituting honey for sugar in preserves. Jams and jellies need sugar and acid to activate the pectin, which is what jells the mixture. The pectin may occur naturally in the fruit, as it does in apples, quince, some varieties of plums, grapes, citrus, and most berries. If the pectin is not naturally present in the fruit it must be added. In either case, without the sugar and acid the product will not set. To use honey when canning fruits with naturally occurring pectin, substitute it for no more than half of the sugar called for in a recipe. In recipes calling for added pectin, honey can be used to replace all of the sugar.

Although I am always one to recommend experimentation, when it comes to jams, jellies, and preserves it is best to follow tried and true recipes until you feel comfortable and then proceed with any experimentation, using as guides the recipes in this book or those that may accompany certain products that you like.

TIPS FOR SUBSTITUTING
HONEY FOR SUGAR

There are no hard and fast rules for substituting honey for sugar, but I have put together some guidelines to help you along. In general, the substitution comes down to a matter of taste. Some people use it cup for cup, while others prefer ½ cup to ⅔ cup of honey per 1 cup of white sugar.

There are several differences to take into consideration when substituting honey for sugar:

- Honey adds moisture that table sugar does not.
- Honey adds its own flavor to the finished product.
- Honey adds acid to a recipe.
- Honey can cause baked foods to brown more quickly.

Moisture   Substituting an equal volume of honey for sugar will likely give you a finished product that is rather soggy and sticky. But if you examine the rest of the ingredients in a recipe, you can determine which items will absorb some of the water in the honey, and increase those to compensate. Or you can take the opposite approach and reduce some of the liquid in the recipe—a good general rule is to reduce the amount of liquid (such as water or milk) by ¼ cup for every cup of honey used.

Flavor   Honey has its own unique flavor. Generally, it is a light and pleasing flavor, and as discussed earlier, the flavor intensity varies greatly between the many varied types of honey. If the flavor of one type of honey is not to your liking and conflicts with the desired taste of your recipe, try substituting a different type of honey. Sometimes you'll need to experiment, or you may decide that a particular recipe does not work for you with a honey substitute.

Acidity   If the recipe you are using is sensitive to the addition of acid, you will have to neutralize the acid that honey adds with a pinch of baking soda. Adding ⅛ teaspoon of baking soda per 1 cup of honey is advised in baking, but since most canning recipes prefer acidity, no action is needed if you are using honey in place of sugar there.

Faster browning   When you have substituted honey for sugar in a recipe, you'll need to watch that it doesn't brown too quickly. Lower the oven temperature about 25 degrees Fahrenheit (20°C) to prevent over-browning.

General recommendations for baking (pies, cakes, cookies, etc.)   Since the type, quality, and properties of the other ingredients in a recipe will affect how the sweetener acts, you may have to do some trial and error to get the exact substitution for the results you want. But these ratios should work and be tasty: Use 1 cup of honey to replace 1 cup of sugar. Reduce other liquids by ¼ cup for each 1 cup of honey you add to the recipe. Lower the oven temperature about 25 degrees Fahrenheit (20°C) to prevent overbrowning.

Obviously, I took into consideration all of the above when creating the recipes in this book. But you can try substituting honey for sugar in almost any recipe you please. It may take a few tries to get the new version just right, but experimentation is part of the fun of cooking!

BRINING FISH AND MEATS

Brining is a very effective method of adding flavor to meat. The meat absorbs the brine, a mixture of salt, water, and other spices/flavorings, which creates a more uniformly seasoned dish. It also results in a wonderfully juicy finished dish. How it works is the salt in the solution draws moisture away from the protein cells in the meat, while at the same time altering their shape. This allows the cells to expand and hold on to more water, basically plumping up the cells. This effect keeps the meat moist, even if it gets slightly overcooked.

The salt also kills any bacteria that might be present and/or prevents them from multiplying, which means that brined meat has less harmful bacteria than meat that has not been brined.

Though most meat brine is based solely on salt, sugar is also a common addition. Sugar in solution is absorbed in the same way as salt is, and helps to balance the excess saltiness. It also results in a darker outer surface or skin of the finished product, whether it is roasted or smoked. I find the addition of honey rather than sugar brings even more flavor and a beautiful exterior color to the finished meat.

One important point to remember when brining meat with sugar in any form is that the product will brown quicker. I suggest reducing the roasting temperature by 25 degrees Fahrenheit (20°C) and cooking the meat for a little longer, until it has reached the desired internal temperature.

Practically any combination of herbs, spices, and flavorings can also be added to basic brine for a variety of fish and meat preparations. I am constantly experimenting with different flavor combinations. Sometimes it's a matter of what I have on hand, like rosemary and sage in fall and winter, when a lot of the tender herbs are not available, or fresh thyme, parsley, basil, and more during the growing season. With fish, tried and true flavors like lemon (usually in slices), garlic, fresh dill, or fennel always work. Of course herbs can always be purchased at any time of the year, but I find they just don't have the flavor intensity that home or locally grown herbs do.

Feel free to experiment with flavorings, and don't be afraid to try different combinations. The worst that can happen is that a combination doesn't work and you try something else. But do keep the following brine times in mind. The longer the product is immersed in the brine, the more seasoned the end result will be.

Basic brine times   The amount of time you leave the meat in the brine is very important. Too long, and the end result will be too salty. It's always better to err on the side of caution. Remember, we are not talking about curing or preserving meat. We are talking about brining meat for roasting and smoking.

These are suggested times. Some trial and error may be required to achieve your preferred results.

Boneless chicken breast	2 hours
Whole chicken legs (drumstick and thigh)	4 hours
Whole chicken, 3½ to 4 pounds (1.5–2 kg)	4 to 6 hours
Whole pork tenderloin, 12 ounces to 1 pound (375–500 g)	3 hours
Whole turkey, 10 to 15 pounds (4–7 kg)	24 hours
Pork chops, 1¼ inch (3.5 cm) thick	2 hours
Pork shoulder or beef roast, 3 to 4 pounds (1.5–2 kg)	8 hours to overnight
Thin fish fillets	1 hour maximum
Thick fish fillets (more than 1 inch thick)	6 to 8 hours

Brined items should be allowed to rest before cooking to ensure a more even distribution of the salt. Depending on the size of the item, resting time should be from 1 to 2 hours or up to 24 hours.

On the page opposite you'll find my recipe for basic honey brine. I haven't specified a type of honey because many different varieties would work wonderfully. For red meat like beef, bison, and even ostrich, which is treated very much like lean beef when cooking, I prefer to use a dark honey, such as buckwheat, chestnut, or blackberry. With lighter meats, such as poultry or pork, or even fish, I prefer to use a lighter honey (just as I would use lighter bodied and flavored wines). Also, as discussed, you can add lots of different flavorings to this recipe, such as fresh herbs, spices, garlic, or chili flakes. Make sure to add them before removing the pot from the heat.

WHAT IS RAW HONEY?

You will notice as you move through this book that I mention and call for raw honey. So what is raw honey? It's pure honey that is unpasteurized—unheated and unprocessed in any way other than straining. It retains its natural characteristics, including minute pollen particles from the blossoms from which it was sourced. Basically, it is honey straight from the hive.

Inside the hive, the bees themselves keep the temperature at just below 100°F (38°C). Unfortunately, most commercial honey products are heated to 155°F (68°C), which destroys many of the helpful enzymes and yeasts that are naturally present. The honey is then further processed through fine filters to remove any other particles and pollen—this produces a clear liquid that is often blended with other honeys before bottling.

Though raw honey is warmed slightly to enable straining, it is never heated beyond 110°F (43°C). This allows the honey to retain its natural flavors, and ensures that valuable heat-sensitive nutrients are protected. Important enzymes such as amylase, which aides in the breakdown and digestion of carbohydrates, are also protected.

BASIC HONEY BRINE

This recipe does have quite a large yield; any extra can be kept in the refrigerator for up to 1 week or even frozen for later use. You can also cut the recipe in half for smaller cuts of meat. To use less brine, simply add the meat to a large resealable freezer bag, add the brine to cover, squeeze out as much air as possible, and seal before refrigerating. This will ensure all surfaces of the meat are in contact with the brine.

MAKES ABOUT 10 CUPS, ENOUGH TO BRINE 1 WHOLE (3½–4 LB) CHICKEN

8 cups water

1 cup pickling or kosher salt

1½ cups honey

Combine the water and salt in a pot on medium heat, and bring to a simmer. Stir until the salt has dissolved, then remove from the heat. Add the honey and stir to combine.

Chill thoroughly before using.

BREAKFAST

28
HONEY-POACHED APPLES AND PEARS

29
BASIC ALMOND CREPES

31
WARM CHOCOLATE ALMOND CREPES
WITH RASPBERRY HONEY BUTTER

34
RICE-FLOUR PANCAKES WITH FRESH BERRIES
AND HONEY YOGURT MINT SAUCE

HONEY-POACHED
APPLES AND PEARS

This is great for breakfast as well as dessert. Almost any varieties of apples and pears can be used, but try to pick ones that will cook in the same amount of time (or stagger the cooking time). Some of my favorite apples for poaching are Gala, Fuji, and Golden Delicious; they all hold up to lengthy cooking. Gravenstein is also very good but only when recently picked as they tend to go mealy. As far as pears go, most varieties can be successfully poached as long as they aren't too ripe. They should give slightly when gently squeezed. Common varieties are Bosc, Bartlett, and Anjou; Asian pears will not work well due to their delicate flavor, which is lost during cooking.

MAKES ABOUT 3½ CUPS

2 cups apple juice or water

¼ cup honey

Zest of 1 large lemon, cut into strips

2 tsp Fruit-Fresh (see Chef's Tip)

1 vanilla bean

2 apples

2 medium-sized ripe pears

Combine the apple juice or water, honey, lemon zest, and Fruit-Fresh in a medium saucepan.

With a sharp knife, split the vanilla bean lengthwise. Scrape out the tiny seeds with the back of a knife. Add the seeds along with the split-open vanilla bean to the saucepan.

Peel and core the apples, and cut each one into 8 pieces, dropping the pieces into the saucepan right after you cut them. Do the same with the pears.

Place the saucepan on medium heat and bring to a simmer. Cook until the apples and pears are tender but still firm, about 3 to 4 minutes.

Remove from the heat, let cool, and serve. Or transfer to a heat-resistant container, and let cool to room temperature before covering and storing in the refrigerator. You can serve these cold in the morning.

CHEF'S TIP
Fruit-Fresh is the most common brand of ascorbic acid color keeper, a powder that prevents the browning of fruits and vegetables.

BASIC ALMOND CREPES

These crepes can be made ahead and used in myriad ways. They are handy for a quick breakfast, or an easy dessert with fillings such as chocolate mousse, whipped cream, or ice cream. Once you've mastered the technique, use two or even three pans at a time to speed up the process. Crepes can be frozen in a stack; just be sure to wrap them tightly.

MAKES 24 CREPES

6 large eggs

⅓ cup honey

2¼ cups milk

1 tsp almond extract

2 cups all-purpose flour

½ cup sliced almonds, toasted and finely ground

¼ cup vegetable oil, plus more for the pan (or use nonstick cooking spray)

In a bowl large enough for all of the ingredients, whisk together the eggs and honey, and then stir in the milk and almond extract. Whisk in the flour ½ cup at a time until smooth. Stir in the ground almonds and oil.

Cover the batter and set aside for 20 to 30 minutes.

Heat a 6-inch nonstick pan on medium heat. Coat lightly with oil (or nonstick cooking spray), and pour about 3 tablespoons of the batter into the middle of the pan, tilting and swirling to coat evenly with the batter.

Cook until the edges start to brown, and then using a thin heatproof spatula, turn the crepe. Cook the other side for 10 to 15 seconds more.

Remove to a plate and repeat with the rest of the batter, stacking the crepes as you go. (They won't stick together.) Allow to cool before serving with a filling.

VARIATIONS

· Substitute other nuts such as hazelnuts or walnuts.
· Add spices such as ground cinnamon, ginger, or nutmeg to the batter.
· Substitute quinoa flour for the wheat flour and toasted quinoa (kept whole) for the ground almonds.

CHEF'S TIP
Sliced almonds will toast more evenly than whole almonds.

WARM CHOCOLATE ALMOND CREPES WITH RASPBERRY HONEY BUTTER

You'll end up with about 1½ cups of Chocolate Hazelnut Spread and 1 cup of Raspberry Honey Butter, more than what is called for in this recipe. In fact, I like to double the chocolate spread; it goes very well on toasted sourdough or with the Honey Fig Bread (page 40), or as a filling for the Hazelnut Sugar Cookies (page 144), or drizzled over ice cream (if you warm it first). The raspberry butter is also great on toasted sourdough, and on warm biscuits, French toast, and pancakes.

SERVES 4

CHOCOLATE HAZELNUT SPREAD

5 oz semisweet or bittersweet chocolate, coarsely chopped

½ cup honey

¼ cup unsalted butter, cut into cubes

¼ cup heavy cream (35%)

1 Tbsp (½ fl oz) hazelnut-flavored liqueur

¼ cup chopped toasted hazelnuts (skins removed; see Chef's Tip on page 131) (optional)

RASPBERRY HONEY BUTTER

½ cup plus 2 Tbsp fresh or frozen raspberries, divided

2 Tbsp honey

Pinch of salt

½ cup unsalted butter, softened

FOR THE CREPES

8 almond crepes (see page 29)

1 cup Chocolate Hazelnut Spread

¼ cup Raspberry Honey Butter

½ cup sweetened whipped cream, for serving

Powdered sugar, for serving

Cocoa powder, for serving

Make the chocolate hazelnut spread   Place the chocolate, honey, butter, and cream in a double boiler or a bowl set over a pot of simmering water on medium heat. Stir frequently until melted and combined, and then remove from the heat. Stir in the liqueur and hazelnuts (if using).

Continued on page 32

Continued from page 31

Set aside about 1 cup for the crepes. Store the rest in a clean jar, and let cool. It will keep for up to 1 month in the refrigerator.

Make the raspberry honey butter   Place ½ cup of the raspberries in a small saucepan on medium heat. Crush with a fork to release some of the juice, and bring to a simmer.

Cook, stirring, until reduced in volume by half. Remove from the heat and press through a fine-meshed sieve into a small bowl. Stir in the honey and salt.

Place the butter into another bowl, and pour the honey mixture overtop. Combine well using a wooden spoon or rubber spatula. Carefully fold in the remaining 2 tablespoons of raspberries.

Divide the mixture in two. Place each portion on a square of plastic wrap or waxed paper and roll into a cylinder. Refrigerate or freeze the rolls until needed. The rolls of butter can be conveniently sliced as needed.

Assemble the crepes   Preheat the oven to 300°F. Lay the crepes flat on a work surface. Divide the Chocolate Hazelnut Spread onto the 8 crepes and spread evenly. Fold the crepes in half and then into quarters. Place on a cookie sheet or ovenproof tray, and warm them in the oven for 5 minutes. Warm 4 ovenproof plates in the oven as well.

Remove the crepes from the oven, and place 2 crepes on each of the plates. Slice the Raspberry Honey Butter into 8 coin-sized pieces; you'll be using about half of one log. Place one coin on each crepe.

Garnish with the whipped cream, and dust the plates with powdered sugar and/or cocoa powder.

Serve while warm and the butter is beginning to melt.

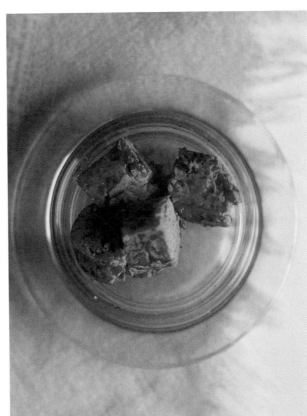

RICE-FLOUR PANCAKES WITH FRESH BERRIES AND HONEY YOGURT MINT SAUCE

A lighter alternative to the usual wheat-flour batter. You can also experiment with different flours such as quinoa, pea, and chickpea—they each bring very distinct flavors to your plate! The yogurt mint sauce is also great with savory dishes; I use less honey (I start with 1 tablespoon and adjust to taste) and serve the sauce with spicy grilled fish, chicken, or lamb.

MAKES TWELVE TO FOURTEEN 3-INCH PANCAKES

1 cup brown-rice flour, more if needed

2 tsp baking powder

1 Tbsp sunflower seeds

1 Tbsp pumpkin seeds

1 Tbsp poppy seeds

2 large eggs, separated

2 Tbsp honey

⅓ cup yogurt

⅓ cup melted butter or vegetable oil, plus more for cooking the pancakes

¼ cup milk, more if needed

½ tsp vanilla extract

1 pint (2 cups) fresh berries (raspberries, blackberries, strawberries, etc.)

HONEY YOGURT MINT SAUCE

½ cup plain yogurt

3 Tbsp honey

2 Tbsp fresh lemon or lime juice

¼ cup chopped fresh mint

Sift together the rice flour and baking powder into a bowl, and then add the sunflower, pumpkin, and poppy seeds.

In a separate bowl, beat the egg whites until firm peaks form.

In a third, large bowl, combine the egg yolks, honey, yogurt, butter or oil, milk, and vanilla. Add the flour mixture and whisk until smooth. Fold in the whipped egg whites. Set aside for 15 minutes.

Make the honey yogurt mint sauce Whisk together all of the ingredients.

Cook the pancakes   Once the batter has rested, add extra milk if it's too thick, or extra rice flour if it's too thin.

Heat a nonstick pan on medium heat. Add the butter or oil and cover the bottom of the pan. Portion ¼-cup scoops of batter onto the hot pan. When bubbles appear on the surface of the pancakes and pop, turn over and cook until lightly browned.

Serve with fresh berries and Honey Yogurt Mint Sauce.

 In its lifetime, a single honeybee brings in enough nectar to make about half a teaspoon of honey.

BREADS

WHOLE-GRAIN HONEY BREAD

This is healthy, hearty bread with a hint of sweetness and a good chewy crust. It is great with strong cheese or as breakfast toast. Whole-grain kernels are available at most health food stores; you can substitute whatever's available. These particular grains all cook in relatively the same amount of time. Kamut is a type of wheat with a much larger kernel.

MAKES 3 LOAVES

½ cup wheat berries

¼ cup hulled barley (not pearl barley)

¼ cup whole kamut kernels

¼ cup whole rye kernels

¼ cup whole oat kernels/groats

4 cups water

½ cup honey

1 Tbsp active dry yeast or instant yeast

¼ cup vegetable or extra-virgin olive oil

2 tsp table salt

1 cup dark rye flour

½ cup ground flaxseed

¼ cup whole flaxseed

3½–4 cups all-purpose or bread flour, plus more for kneading

1 large egg

Place the 5 types of whole grains in a dry heavy-bottomed stockpot on medium heat, and toast until lightly colored and aromatic. Add the water, bring to a simmer, and cook at a light simmer, lowering the heat if necessary, for 45 minutes to 1 hour or until the grains are tender. Remove from the heat and cool until the cooking liquid is just warm (no more than 110°F). Strain, reserving 2 cups of the cooking liquid. Pour the cooking liquid into a large mixing bowl, and stir in the honey, and the yeast if using active dry yeast. (See Chef's Tip.) Let stand for 5 to 10 minutes.

Add the grains to the honey and yeast, and then add the oil, salt, rye flour, and ground and whole flaxseed, and stir until smooth. Add the all-purpose or bread flour, and work it in until you have a ball.

Turn out the dough onto a lightly floured work surface, and knead for 6 to 8 minutes until relatively smooth, adding just enough flour to the work surface to keep the dough from sticking. Place it in an oiled bowl, cover with a damp cloth or plastic wrap, and set aside in a warm place. Let rise until doubled in size, about 2 hours.

Turn out the dough onto a floured surface, and knead briefly. Divide the dough into 3 portions, and form each into a round loaf. Place on a greased and floured baking sheet, cover, and let rise to one and a half times the original size, about 1½ to 2 hours. (The loaves can also be placed in 8½- × 4½-inch loaf pans.)

Preheat the oven to 375°F.

Whisk together the egg with 2 tablespoons of water. Brush the loaves with the egg wash, and bake for 40 to 45 minutes. Remove from the oven and turn out onto a wire rack to cool.

CHEF'S TIP

If using instant yeast, add the yeast to the all-purpose flour just before mixing it in.

HONEY FIG BREAD

This bread is wonderful with soft cheeses such as chèvre, Brie, and Camembert, and is also delicious toasted, especially when drizzled with a little extra honey. A great way to use up the last few slices is to make French toast with them!

MAKES TWO 8½- × 4½-INCH LOAVES

6 cups bread flour, plus more
   for kneading

1 Tbsp instant yeast

2 tsp table salt

2 Tbsp honey

¼ cup extra-virgin olive oil

2 large eggs, divided

1 cup warm water

1 cup finely chopped dried figs

2 Tbsp milk

⅓ cup crushed sliced almonds

Combine the flour, yeast, and salt in a large bowl. (Use the bowl of an electric stand mixer, if you have one.) In a small bowl, whisk together the honey, olive oil, 1 egg, and warm water. Add to the flour mixture. Mix using a wooden spoon (or the bread hook of the stand mixer) until thoroughly combined.

Scrape out the dough onto a lightly floured work surface, and knead for 6 to 8 minutes or until smooth and elastic, adding just enough flour to the work surface to keep the dough from sticking.

Place in an oiled bowl, cover with a damp cloth or plastic wrap, and keep in a warm spot until doubled in volume, about 1 hour.

Turn out the dough onto a floured work surface, and knead briefly. Flatten into a rough rectangle, about ¾ to 1 inch thick, and top with the figs. Fold over the dough, and knead for 1 to 2 minutes to incorporate the figs into the dough. Divide it in half. Form each half into a ball.

Cover and set aside for 2 to 3 minutes. Grease and flour two 8½- × 4½-inch loaf pans. Shape the dough balls into ovals and press into the pans. Cover and let rise in a warm spot until one and a half times the size, about 30 to 40 minutes.

Preheat the oven to 375°F.

Whisk together the remaining egg and the milk. Brush the tops of each loaf with the egg mixture, and sprinkle with the crushed almonds. Bake for 40 minutes.

Remove from the pans and cool on a wire rack.

 A worker bee can only sting once—her stinger is torn from her body (and left in the victim), and she dies soon after. Drones (male bees) do not have stingers. The queen bee's stinger is barbless so it does not tear away from her body when used for stinging, which is rarely if ever.

ROSEMARY, HONEY, AND CORNMEAL SCONES

The texture of these scones is very different from traditional scones. The extra yolk gives them a cakelike crumb, and the cornmeal adds a bit of crunch. These are best while still warm from the oven; a little extra honey drizzled overtop doesn't hurt either. The scones will spread a bit as they bake. To make the scones rise higher, bake them in a metal ring mold, or fashion one using aluminum foil and a paper clip.

MAKES TWELVE 3-INCH WEDGES

1¾ cups all-purpose flour

4 tsp baking powder

¼ tsp table salt

1 cup white or yellow cornmeal,
  plus more for sprinkling

1 Tbsp finely chopped fresh rosemary

2 large eggs

3 Tbsp honey

¾ cup milk

¼ cup extra-virgin olive oil

Preheat the oven to 350°F.

Into a bowl, sift together the flour, baking powder, and salt, and then mix in the cornmeal and rosemary. Separate one of the eggs, putting the egg yolk in a bowl, reserving the egg white for later. Add the remaining egg to the egg yolk along with the honey, milk, and olive oil, and whisk together.

Pour this mixture into the dry ingredients, and mix with a wooden spoon until combined. A few spots of unmixed flour are fine. You don't want to overmix or the scones will be tough.

Turn out the dough onto a lightly floured work surface, knead the dough slightly, and divide in half. Shape each piece into a 6-inch round, and place onto a nonstick or greased baking sheet. For each round, make deep cuts so you'll have 6 wedges (but do not separate the wedges).

Whisk the reserved egg white with 1 tablespoon of water, and brush each round lightly. Sprinkle with a little cornmeal, and bake for 20 to 25 minutes.

Serve warm with butter and honey.

QUINOA, CORNMEAL, AND PEA-FLOUR BISCUITS

Because these biscuits do not contain wheat flour and therefore lack the structure that gluten provides, they may come out a little denser than you're used to. Luckily the unique flavor of pea flour makes up for it. This and quinoa flour can be found in most large supermarkets and health food stores.

MAKES TWELVE 2-INCH BISCUITS

⅔ cup quinoa flour

⅔ cup pea flour

1 Tbsp baking powder

½ tsp table salt

⅔ cup yellow cornmeal, plus more
   for dusting work surface

½ cup cold unsalted butter or lard

¾ cup milk or rice milk

1 large egg

2 Tbsp buckwheat honey

Preheat the oven to 400°F.

Sift the quinoa flour, pea flour, baking powder, and salt into a mixing bowl. Add the cornmeal and mix well. Cut in the cold butter or lard using a pastry blender or two butter knives, distributing the fat throughout and leaving some pieces that are pea-sized and larger.

In a separate bowl, whisk together the milk, egg, and honey.

Make a well in the center of the flour mixture, and pour in the milk mixture. Using a spatula or your hands, gently fold the ingredients and gather into a ball.

Turn out the mixture onto a work surface dusted with cornmeal, and knead a few times to combine. Flatten the dough into a disk 1 inch thick, and using a biscuit cutter or cookie cutter, cut into your desired biscuit shape.

Place the biscuits on a nonstick or greased and floured baking sheet and bake for 10 minutes.

Serve warm with butter and honey.

PIZZA DOUGH

The key to a good pizza is the dough, whose flavor and texture are improved if the dough is allowed to rest and develop slowly in the fridge. Make it 2 to 3 days ahead if possible; the extra time allows the yeasts and proteins to develop. Other tips: limit the number of toppings (three at the most), go easy on the cheese, and don't forget to season the pizza well.

MAKES 1½ LB OF DOUGH, ENOUGH FOR THREE 10-INCH OR TWO 12-INCH PIZZAS

4½ cups bread flour, plus more
   for kneading
2 Tbsp instant yeast
2 tsp table salt

1 cup warm water
2 Tbsp buckwheat or other
   dark honey
2 Tbsp extra-virgin olive oil

Combine the flour, yeast, and salt in a mixing bowl. Combine the water, honey, and olive oil in a measuring cup, and stir into the flour mixture. Stir with a wooden spoon to form a rough dough.

Turn out the dough onto a lightly floured work surface. Knead the dough until smooth and elastic, 5 to 6 minutes, adding just enough flour to the work surface to prevent the dough from sticking.

Place the dough in a clean, lightly floured bowl, and cover with a damp cloth or plastic wrap. Set aside in a warm spot until doubled in size, 45 to 60 minutes.

CHEF'S TIP

The dough can also be placed in the refrigerator after kneading for up to 3 days, to improve the texture and flavor of the final pizza crust. Cover with plastic wrap instead of a damp cloth.

LITTLE BITES

48
SPICED HONEY-GLAZED ALMONDS

50
FRESH FIG AND BRIE BRUSCHETTA

51
FIVE-SPICE HONEY-GLAZED MEATBALLS

52
HONEY-BRINED BEEF JERKY

55
MINI PORK AND CHICKEN SATAY
WITH HONEY PEANUT SAUCE

58
SOY CHICKEN WINGS

60
TEA-SMOKED SCALLOPS WITH
HONEY ORANGE MARMALADE

62
GRILLED BACON-WRAPPED HALIBUT
AND SALMON SKEWERS

64
CANADIAN WHISKY AND HONEY—CURED SALMON

SPICED HONEY-GLAZED ALMONDS

You may want to make an extra batch of these for backup as they will disappear quickly. Any variety of whole nuts will work well in this recipe.

MAKES ABOUT 6½ CUPS

½ cup paprika

3 Tbsp cayenne pepper

2 tsp ground ginger

2 tsp ground cumin

½ cup honey

2 large egg whites

2 tsp liquid smoke

1 Tbsp kosher salt

2½ lb whole almonds

Preheat the oven to 275°F.

Sift together the paprika, cayenne, ginger, and cumin into a bowl.

In a bowl large enough to hold the almonds, whisk together the honey, egg whites, liquid smoke, and salt until slightly foamy. Add the almonds and toss to coat.

Sprinkle the spice mixture into the bowl. Toss to coat the nuts evenly.

Spread out onto parchment paper–lined baking sheets. Try to separate the nuts to keep them from sticking to each other.

Bake for approximately 20 to 30 minutes or until the coating is dry and crispy. Remove and cool completely on the baking sheets. Store in an airtight container.

FRESH FIG AND
BRIE BRUSCHETTA

This is not so much a recipe as an idea for a simple starter for a casual summer meal. I also love to have savory-and-sweet items such as this as a little breakfast to start my day. This dish is open to all kinds of variations—try using other fresh fruits that are naturally very sweet, such as peaches and pears, and any soft cheese. Blue versions such as Cambozola also work well. The key is to balance sweet, salty, and creamy. Use only good-quality ingredients here: homemade bread, if possible; a good olive oil; tender, seasonal figs; and your favorite local honey.

SERVES 4

4 large slices crusty Italian, French, or sourdough bread

Extra-virgin olive oil, for drizzling

About 4 oz Brie (or Camembert) cheese, thinly sliced

4 fresh figs or to taste, sliced

Honey, for drizzling

Coarse sea salt

Toast the bread lightly, and drizzle with olive oil. Top with the cheese slices and then with the figs. Drizzle with honey. Finally top with just a few grains of sea salt.

FIVE-SPICE HONEY-GLAZED MEATBALLS

Serve with decorative toothpicks as an informal hors d'oeuvre. For a main course, place the meatballs on a bed of "Asian slaw"—I like to shred Chinese cabbage, carrot, and green onion, and toss it with a dressing made of three parts vegetable oil, one part rice vinegar, one part soy sauce, and a touch of honey and sesame oil.

MAKES 24 MEATBALLS; SERVES 6 AS AN APPETIZER

½ lb lean ground pork

½ lb ground turkey

1 large egg, beaten

1 Tbsp soy sauce

1 Tbsp minced garlic

1 Tbsp minced fresh ginger

2 tsp five-spice powder, divided

5 Tbsp brown-rice flour, divided

Vegetable oil, for frying

2 Tbsp toasted sesame seeds

2 Tbsp chopped fresh cilantro

SAUCE

¼ cup honey

2 cloves garlic, minced

1 Tbsp minced fresh ginger

2 Tbsp soy sauce

1 Tbsp fresh lime juice

Combine the pork, turkey, egg, soy sauce, garlic, ginger, 1 teaspoon of the five-spice, and 2 tablespoons of the rice flour in a bowl. Refrigerate for 30 minutes.

Moisten the palms of your hands with cold water and form the mixture into 24 balls. Place the remaining rice flour and five-spice on a plate and mix it together. Roll the meatballs in the flour to coat, and refrigerate.

Place enough oil in a heavy-bottomed frying pan to cover the bottom. Heat on medium and fry the meatballs in batches, about 5 minutes. Turn the meatballs to brown evenly. Remove from the pan and drain on paper towels. After frying all of the meatballs, clean the pan.

For the sauce, combine the honey, garlic, ginger, and soy sauce in the cleaned pan and bring to a simmer on medium heat. Add the meatballs, turning them carefully to coat. Cook for 3 to 4 minutes to heat through, and then stir in the lime juice.

Add the sesame seeds and cilantro, toss to coat, and serve.

HONEY-BRINED BEEF JERKY

Drying meat was traditionally a preservation method, to ensure a food source in times of scarcity. These days we usually dry meat because we enjoy the taste! Jerky is a good high-protein source of energy, making it an ideal item to bring along when you go hiking or camping. If you have a smoker, by all means use it instead of a dehydrator.

MAKES ABOUT 1 LB

2 lb lean beef (see Chef's Tips)

2 cups cooled Basic Honey Brine (see page 25)

¼ cup red wine (see Chef's Tips)

¼ cup honey

1 Tbsp red chili flakes or to taste

4 cloves garlic, minced

EQUIPMENT

Food dehydrator or oven with a dehydration mode

Slice the beef on a bias and across the grain into 6-inch strips approximately ⅛ to ¼ inch thick. (Slicing across the grain makes the jerky more tender and easier to chew.)

Trim and discard any excess fat and sinew from the strips, and place in a nonreactive container (glass, stainless steel, or ceramic) just large enough for all of the ingredients. Add the brine, wine, honey, chili flakes, and garlic, and mix well. (Alternatively, place all of the ingredients in a large freezer bag. Press out all of the air and seal.) Cover and refrigerate for 8 hours or overnight.

Drain the meat well through a fine-meshed sieve, allowing the chili flakes and garlic to remain on the meat. Pat the meat dry on a clean kitchen towel or on paper towels.

Coat the racks of the dehydrator with nonstick cooking spray. If you're using an oven, coat a stainless-steel wire rack with nonstick cooking spray, and place the rack on a baking sheet. Lay the strips of meat on the rack, close to each other but not touching.

Set your dehydrator to 140°F to 145°F, or turn on the dehydration mode of your oven. Drying will take up to 8 hours depending on the thickness of the slices, the leanness of the meat, and the humidity and temperature. (It may help to have the oven door propped open slightly to remove excess moisture from the oven.) The jerky is sufficiently dried when the fibers break when bent completely, but it should still be pliable.

Store in an airtight container in the refrigerator for up to 2 weeks or in the freezer for up to 6 months.

VARIATION

Use venison instead of beef, adding extra flavorings such as juniper berries and/or dried thyme, oregano, or rosemary to the brine.

CHEF'S TIPS

· The most economical cuts are beef shoulder and from the hip (including bottom round, eye of round, and top round).

· Use a red wine that you'd also drink—as I'd recommend for all recipes.

MINI PORK AND CHICKEN SATAY WITH HONEY PEANUT SAUCE

Although these little skewers make for a great cocktail item, they can easily be made larger and served as a starter or part of a buffet.

MAKES 24 SKEWERS; SERVES 6–8 AS AN APPETIZER

2 boneless, skinless chicken breasts, each cut into 12 (1-inch) cubes

1½ lb lean pork leg, cut into 24 (1-inch) cubes

1 Tbsp minced fresh ginger

1 Tbsp minced garlic

1 Thai chili, seeded and minced

2 tsp ground coriander seeds

1 tsp ground fennel seeds

2 tsp toasted sesame oil

2 tsp honey

Pinch of salt

Fresh lime wedges, for serving

HONEY PEANUT SAUCE

2 Tbsp vegetable oil, divided

1½ cups (6 oz) blanched peanuts

1 small onion, chopped

2 cloves garlic, minced

1 Tbsp chopped fresh ginger

1 Thai chili, seeded and chopped

¾ cup coconut milk, more if needed

2 Tbsp soy sauce

2 Tbsp honey

1 Tbsp fresh lime juice or to taste, more if needed

EQUIPMENT

24 (4- to 5-inch-long) bamboo skewers

Soak the bamboo skewers in warm water for several hours or overnight. Thread one cube of chicken and one cube of pork onto each skewer. With the back of a heavy knife or cleaver, flatten the pork and chicken slightly.

In a shallow dish or container, place the skewers in a single layer. In a bowl, combine the ginger, garlic, chili, coriander, fennel, sesame oil, honey, and salt, and then pour the mixture over the skewers. Cover and refrigerate for 2 hours.

Continued on page 56

Continued from page 55

Make the honey peanut sauce   Heat a wok or frying pan on medium and add 1 tablespoon of the oil. Add the peanuts and stir constantly for 1 to 2 minutes to toast. Turn the peanuts out onto a plate.

Add the remaining tablespoon of oil to the pan. Add the onion, garlic, ginger, and chili, and cook on medium heat, stirring, for 30 seconds. Add the coconut milk, soy sauce, honey, lime juice, and toasted peanuts, and bring to a simmer. Cook until slightly thickened and remove from the heat.

Cool slightly, and using a blender or food processor, blend until smooth. If the sauce is too thick, thin with extra coconut milk and lime juice.

Grill the satay   Heat a charcoal or gas grill to medium-high, or turn on the broiler of the oven (the satay should be 2 to 3 inches away from the element). Place the skewers on the grill or, if using a broiler, on a foil-lined tray. Cook for 2 to 3 minutes on each side.

Serve with the lime wedges and with the Honey Peanut Sauce on the side for dipping.

SOY CHICKEN WINGS

You can also use this delicious marinade for pork, beef, or fish. Simmering the wings here results in a simple stock that you can use in any recipe calling for a light chicken stock.

SERVES 4 AS AN APPETIZER

2½ lb chicken wings

1 stalk celery, chopped

1 carrot, chopped

1 small onion, chopped

1 bay leaf

1 Tbsp finely grated fresh ginger

1 Tbsp finely grated garlic

1 tsp sambal oelek or to taste
  (see Chef's Tip)

¼ cup low-sodium Japanese soy sauce

¼ cup honey

½ tsp toasted sesame oil

½ tsp five-spice powder

2 Tbsp rice wine

¼ cup toasted sesame seeds,
  for serving

Rinse the chicken wings and pat dry, and then place them in a stockpot. If you've bought chicken wings that haven't been separated into drumettes and mini-wings, trim off the wing tips and add to the stockpot. You'll also have to cut the chicken wings in half at the joint before adding to the stockpot.

Cover with cold water and bring to a simmer on medium heat. Add the celery, carrot, onion, and bay leaf to the pot, and simmer for 20 to 30 minutes or until tender.

Remove the wings and set aside (but keep the wing tips in the stock if you have them). Continue simmering the stock for 2 hours. Strain through a colander, reserving the stock. Cool and refrigerate or freeze to use for another recipe.

Combine the ginger, garlic, sambal oelek, soy sauce, honey, sesame oil, five-spice, and rice wine in a large container. Add the wings and marinate for 20 minutes.

Preheat the oven to 400°F.

Remove the wings from the marinade, and place on a foil- or parchment paper–lined baking sheet. Place in the oven, and brush every 5 minutes with the marinade. The wings will take about 20 minutes.

Remove from the oven and sprinkle with the sesame seeds.

CHEF'S TIP

Sambal oelek is an Indonesian chili paste preserved with vinegar.

TEA-SMOKED SCALLOPS WITH HONEY ORANGE MARMALADE

You can use this method to smoke a variety of items such as prawns or shrimp, chicken breasts, small fish fillets, or even vegetables. Have some fun and experiment with different marinades and smoking ingredients. Serve these scallops with fresh greens as a formal appetizer or a main course. You can also use smaller scallops (or cut them to size) and place a scallop and some marmalade on firm crackers or chips to serve with cocktails.

SERVES 4 AS AN APPETIZER OR 2 AS A MAIN COURSE

8 (U-10) scallops (see Chef's Tips)
½ cup Basic Honey Brine (see page 25)
1 Tbsp finely grated fresh ginger
2 tsp finely grated garlic
2 whole star anise
2 Tbsp low-sodium soy sauce

ORANGE MARMALADE
2 large oranges (washed well)
1 lemon (washed well)
¼ cup seasoned Japanese rice vinegar
¼ cup honey
Pinch of salt

TEA SMOKE
¼ cup loose-leaf black tea
¼ cup uncooked white rice
Zest of 1 orange, cut into
    ¼-inch-wide strips
1 whole star anise
2 Tbsp brown sugar

EQUIPMENT
Wok with a tight-fitting lid
Round wire rack

Remove the side-muscles from the scallops if present (see Chef's Tips), and place the scallops in a freezer bag. Add the brine, ginger, garlic, star anise, and soy sauce to the bag. Press out as much air as possible, and seal the bag. Refrigerate for 2 hours.

Make the marmalade With a sharp knife or vegetable peeler, remove the rind from the oranges in strips. Lay each strip flat on a work surface, and remove all of the white pith from the inside of the rind. Repeat the process with the lemon. Slice the orange and lemon rinds into very thin strips, and place into a saucepan with the rice vinegar. Bring to a low simmer on low heat and cook until the vinegar has reduced by half, about 20 to 30 minutes.

While the vinegar is reducing, remove any remaining white pith from the oranges. Working over a colander or sieve set over a bowl, cut in between the membranes of the oranges to release the individual segments. Squeeze what remains of the orange. Repeat with the lemon. Set aside the orange and lemon segments.

Add all of the accumulated juice to the pan, and continue to reduce at a low simmer until the orange and lemon rinds are tender. Remove from the heat, stir in the honey and salt, and set aside.

Smoke the scallops Line the wok with foil, and place all of the smoking ingredients in the bottom. Spray the wire rack with nonstick cooking spray and set aside.

Remove the scallops from the brine, rinse under cold water, and pat dry. Place the scallops on the rack and set aside.

Heat the wok on medium and cover tightly. Have a wet towel ready. When the smoke begins to accumulate, reduce the heat to low, and place the rack with the scallops into the wok. Cover the wok with the lid, and place the wet towel around the edges to keep in the smoke.

Smoke on low heat for approximately 5 to 6 minutes. The scallops should still be a little soft when done.

Remove the scallops from the wok and portion onto individual plates. Top each scallop with a spoonful of marmalade, garnish with the reserved orange and lemon segments, and serve.

CHEF'S TIPS

· U-10 refers to the number of scallops per pound; *U* stands for "under," in this case under 10 scallops per pound.

· The side-muscle is the small bit of muscle tissue that attaches the scallop to the shell. Although edible, it can be tough and chewy.

GRILLED BACON-WRAPPED HALIBUT AND SALMON SKEWERS

This dish lets you serve two different kinds of fish at once! If you have special main ingredients that are fresh and in season, you want them to shine without being overpowered by the other flavors; this recipe is a good example.

SERVES 4 AS AN APPETIZER OR 2 AS A MAIN COURSE

1 (6 oz) halibut fillet (skin removed)

1 (6 oz) salmon fillet (skin removed)

1 Tbsp chopped fresh Italian parsley

1 Tbsp chopped fresh oregano

1 Tbsp chopped fresh rosemary

1 large clove garlic

1 tsp minced lemon zest

½ tsp freshly ground black pepper

Pinch of salt

1 Tbsp extra-virgin olive oil

4 slices bacon (or pancetta)

1 Tbsp fresh lemon juice

1 Tbsp honey

EQUIPMENT

4 bamboo or metal skewers

Cut the halibut fillet into 8 equal-sized cubes; do the same with the salmon fillet. Combine the herbs and garlic and mince together. Add the fish and the herbs to a bowl, along with the lemon zest, pepper, salt, and olive oil. Gently toss to coat.

Lay the bacon on a work surface. Place 2 pieces of the halibut and 2 pieces of the salmon in a row on one end of a slice of bacon. If any herb mixture remains in the bowl, sprinkle a little of it on the pieces of fish. Fold the bacon over the fish pieces. Skewer the pieces and the ends of the bacon. Repeat with the remaining fish and bacon. If you're using pancetta, fold it over the fish and create a rectangular packet, and then insert the skewer. Refrigerate until needed.

Heat a charcoal or gas grill to medium to medium-high heat. Oil the grates well (soak a paper towel with some oil, and using tongs or your grill cleaning brush, rub it evenly over the grates). Combine the lemon juice and honey in a small bowl, and keep it next to the grill with a basting brush.

Pat the bacon-wrapped skewers dry, and place on the grill. Cook for 2 to 3 minutes and turn. Brush with the lemon-honey mixture and cover the grill. Cook for 2 to 3 minutes more or until the fish pieces just begin to flake. Brush with the remaining lemon-honey mixture and serve.

 CHEF'S TIP
If you're using bamboo or other wooden skewers, be sure to soak them in water for several hours or overnight to help prevent them from burning.

CANADIAN WHISKY AND HONEY–CURED SALMON

Serve this as you would gravlax or smoked salmon. The dressing is a good example of how something doesn't have to be complicated to taste good. Adjust the honey-to-mustard ratio according to your taste.

MAKES 2–2½ LB CURED SALMON

1 (2½–3 lb) salmon fillet, skin on

2–3 Tbsp crushed black peppercorns

½ cup plus 1 Tbsp kosher or
  pickling salt

1 cup honey

¼ cup (2 fl oz) Canadian rye whisky

HONEY-MUSTARD DRESSING

3 Tbsp honey

3 Tbsp Dijon mustard

1–2 Tbsp strained brine

Rinse the salmon under cold water and pat dry. With a pair of tweezers, remove the pin bones. Rub the crushed peppercorns into the flesh of the fillet. Place the fillet in a baking dish (glass, stainless steel, or ceramic) that's just large enough to hold the fillet.

Combine the salt, honey, and whisky; the salt does not need to dissolve. Pour over the fillet. Turn the fillet over a few times to coat, ending with the flesh side up.

Lay a large piece of plastic wrap right on top of the salmon and top with a flat tray or plate. Top that with a 4- to 5-pound weight such as a few large cans or a brick.

Refrigerate for 24 hours. Halfway through the curing time, baste the salmon with the liquid, and then replace the weight. The salmon will expel some liquid to form a brine. It is important that the fillet be immersed in as much brine as possible as this is what will cure the salmon. If there isn't enough brine, baste the salmon often.

After 24 hours, check to see that the salmon is fully cured. The flesh should be quite firm. If it still feels soft, return to the brine and cure for another 12 to 24 hours. Once fully cured, remove the salmon from the brine, rinse under cold water, and pat dry. Strain the brine and reserve 1 or 2 tablespoons for the dressing.

To make the dressing, combine the honey and mustard. Thin to desired consistency with the brine. Slice the salmon very thinly on a bias, and serve with the dressing on the side.

 Larger than the female worker bee, the male honeybee (also called a drone) has a single purpose: to mate with the queen. In fact, before winter or when food becomes scarce, female honeybees usually force surviving males out of the nest.

SIDE DISHES

SESAME-HONEY EGG NOODLES

Feel free to add fresh snow peas, bean sprouts, and/or broccoli after cooking the garlic and ginger in the oil. Quickly sauté before adding the honey. And of course you can spice up these noodles by adding hot sauce. Serve with other Asian-inspired dishes such as Five-Spice Honey-Glazed Meatballs (page 51), Honey-Glazed Flank Steak (page 104), and Soy Chicken Wings (page 58).

SERVES 4

½ lb dried Asian egg noodles

2 Tbsp vegetable oil

2 medium cloves garlic, minced

1 Tbsp minced fresh ginger

2 Tbsp honey

2 Tbsp low-sodium soy sauce

Juice of ½ lime or to taste

1 Tbsp toasted sesame oil

¼ cup toasted sesame seeds

Bring a 4-quart pot of salted water to a boil. Add the noodles, and cook following the package instructions.

While the noodles are cooking, prepare the sauce. Heat a 12-inch frying pan on medium and add the vegetable oil. Add the garlic and ginger and stir briefly, and then add the honey and cook for 1 to 2 minutes. Add the soy sauce and lime juice.

Drain the noodles and add to the pan. Toss to coat evenly with the sauce. Add the sesame oil and sesame seeds.

 A single bee flies about 500 miles (800 km) in her lifetime.

STEAMED GREEN BEANS WITH ALMOND HONEY BUTTER

This recipe also works well with other firm vegetables such as broccoli, gai lan (Chinese broccoli), and cauliflower.

SERVES 4–6

1 lb fresh green beans

2 Tbsp extra-virgin olive oil

2 Tbsp unsalted butter

1 cup (4 oz) sliced blanched almonds

¼ tsp sea salt

¼ tsp freshly ground black pepper

Pinch of ground nutmeg or to taste

1 Tbsp dark honey such as buckwheat

Grated zest of 1 lemon

Juice of ½ lemon or to taste

Wash and trim the beans by cutting off the stem ends. (If the beans are fresh, there is no need to trim the tips.) Place in a steamer set over simmering water, and steam for 4 to 5 minutes or until tender and still bright green.

While the beans are steaming, heat a medium-sized frying pan on medium, and add the olive oil and butter. Add the sliced almonds, and stir to coat. Cook, stirring, until the almonds are just beginning to brown.

Add the steamed beans, salt, pepper, nutmeg, honey, and lemon zest, and toss to coat. Serve immediately, adding the lemon juice right before serving (to prevent discoloration).

HONEY-ROASTED PARSNIPS

You can also substitute potatoes for the parsnips, or try combining the two. This makes a delicious accompaniment to roasted or grilled meats.

SERVES 6–8

2 lb parsnips (about 4–6 medium-sized)

1 whole head garlic

6 large sprigs fresh rosemary

3 Tbsp extra-virgin olive oil

¼ cup honey

½ cup water

1 Tbsp smoked paprika

1 tsp table salt

1 tsp freshly ground black pepper

Preheat the oven to 375°F.

Peel the parsnips. Trim off the ends and cut into ½-inch pieces. Separate the cloves of garlic and peel.

Combine all of the ingredients in a roasting pan. (You can keep the rosemary sprigs whole.) Roast in the oven for 20 to 30 minutes or until tender, turning every 10 minutes.

ROASTED BEETS WITH ORANGE AND HONEY GLAZE

If you can find beets with the greens still attached, buy them. Healthy-looking greens mean that the beets are fresh. They'll also make a delicious second side dish. In a large frying pan, add 2 tablespoons of olive oil, 3 to 4 whole garlic cloves, and the greens (cut into 2-inch lengths). Add salt and pepper, 1 teaspoon of red chili flakes, and about ½ cup of water. Cover and cook on medium heat until tender.

SERVES 4–6

1 lb medium-sized red beets, or about 3 lb with tops on

1 Tbsp extra-virgin olive oil

1 whole head garlic

Grated zest and juice of 1 large orange

¾ cup light chicken or vegetable stock

¼ cup dark honey such as buckwheat

4–5 sprigs fresh thyme

1 Tbsp cold unsalted butter

Preheat the oven to 350°F.

Wash the beets well and trim off the tops (if still attached) and roots. Rub the beets with the olive oil and season with salt and freshly ground black pepper. Separate the cloves of garlic, and trim off the root ends, leaving the skins on.

Wrap the beets and garlic cloves in foil (making a large pouch), and place on a baking sheet. Roast the beets for 2 hours or until tender when poked with a knife.

Remove from the oven and cool until they're easy to handle. The skins should come off easily with a little help from a paring knife. Cut each beet into 6 or 8 wedges. Squeeze out the garlic, which should be tender and soft, from the skins.

Place the beets and garlic in a frying pan, and add the orange zest and juice and the stock. Bring to a simmer on medium heat, and cook until the stock has reduced by about three-quarters (that is, only one-quarter of the juice and stock left). Add the honey.

Strip the leaves from the sprigs of thyme, and add to the pan with salt and freshly ground black pepper to taste. Add the butter and swirl just to coat the beets. The beets will be coated with a glaze with very little liquid left in the pan.

HONEY AND BALSAMIC–GLAZED SHALLOTS

This makes a great accompaniment to rich meat dishes, especially grilled meats. Adjust the herbs to suit personal taste; sage, rosemary, or fresh fennel fronds are all good options.

SERVES 6–8

1–2 Tbsp extra-virgin olive oil

1 lb whole shallots, peeled

2 whole heads garlic, cloves
   separated and peeled

1 cup chicken stock

½ cup balsamic vinegar,
   plus more to taste

⅓ cup honey, plus more to taste

1 small bunch fresh thyme or to taste

½ tsp table salt

¼ tsp freshly ground black pepper

1 Tbsp cold unsalted butter

Heat the oil in a frying pan on medium. Add the shallots, garlic, stock, balsamic vinegar, honey, thyme, and salt and pepper, and bring to a low simmer.

Cook, covered, checking every 10 minutes to ensure the liquid hasn't evaporated. (If it has, add a small amount of chicken stock or water.) As the liquid thickens to become a syrup, add more balsamic and/or honey if desired. Coat the shallots and garlic in the liquid.

When the shallots are close to being done, remove the lid, increase the heat to medium, and allow the liquid to reduce to an even thicker syrup that will coat the shallots. The shallots should take approximately 25 to 30 minutes to become tender, depending on their size.

Swirl in the butter and serve.

 Bees can fly up to 5 miles (8 km) from the hive and then turn and head for home in a straight line.

GRILLED RADICCHIO WITH HONEY, GARLIC, AND PINE NUTS

Radicchio is a red endive that is very popular in Italy and the rest of Europe, and widely available in our local markets here. It makes a delicious addition to a salad. One common variety is round and about half the size of a head of iceberg lettuce, and another is made up of elongated leaves similar in shape to romaine lettuce (which makes a good substitute in this recipe). Its unique flavor, often described as bitter, blends well with sweet. Serve this dish warm to accompany grilled or roasted meats, or serve at room temperature as part of an antipasto platter.

SERVES 4

2 medium-sized heads radicchio

4–6 Tbsp extra-virgin olive oil, divided

½ tsp freshly ground black pepper

2 cloves garlic

½ tsp table salt

½ cup dark honey such as buckwheat

1 Tbsp balsamic vinegar

¼ cup toasted pine nuts

Wash the radicchio well in cold water. Trim the root ends of any brown spots and remove any wilted or discolored leaves. Cut the heads in half, through the stem to ensure the leaves stay intact. Lay the radicchio halves cut side up on a tray.

Drizzle with 2 to 3 tablespoons of the olive oil and season with the pepper.

On a cutting board, coarsely chop the garlic and sprinkle it with the salt. Combine, making a smooth paste, using the side of a large knife. Gently rub the garlic paste all over the radicchio to coat.

Combine the remaining 2 to 3 tablespoons of olive oil, the honey, and the balsamic vinegar in a small bowl.

Heat a charcoal or gas grill to medium. Place the radicchio on the grill cut side down. Grill for 2 to 3 minutes until the edges begin to brown. Turn over and grill for 2 to 3 minutes more.

Arrange on a serving platter, drizzle with the olive oil–honey mixture, and sprinkle with the toasted pine nuts.

MAIN DISHES

HONEY-MUSTARD
BEER-BATTERED FISH FILLET

Although lean fish, such as halibut and cod, is usually recommended for deep-frying, certain lean species of salmon (sockeye, coho, and pink) do equally well. Pink salmon's milder flavor makes it a good choice for those who usually find salmon too rich or strong. This is a good deep-fry batter for cooking in batches as it stays crisp. You can also try a mixed fry using an assortment of fish and shellfish; this is enough batter for approximately 1 pound of seafood.

SERVES 4

HONEY-MUSTARD BEER SAUCE

2 Tbsp Dijon mustard

2 Tbsp honey

1 Tbsp fresh lemon juice

¼ cup (2 fl oz) honey lager beer

Salt and freshly ground black pepper,
    to taste

HONEY-MUSTARD BEER BATTER

¾ cup (6 fl oz) cold honey lager beer

1 Tbsp fresh lemon juice

1 Tbsp Dijon mustard

1 tsp table salt

¾ cup all-purpose flour

1½ tsp baking powder

2 Tbsp cornstarch

2 Tbsp yellow mustard seeds

1 lb fish fillets (cod, halibut, salmon, etc.)

2 Tbsp fresh lemon juice

Vegetable oil, for deep-frying

½ cup all-purpose flour

Lemon wedges, for serving

Make the honey-mustard beer sauce In a small bowl, whisk together all of the ingredients. Set aside.

Make the honey-mustard beer batter Combine the beer, lemon juice, mustard, and salt in a small bowl. Sift the flour, baking powder, and cornstarch into another bowl. Add the mustard seeds and combine.

Pour in the beer mixture and mix with a wooden spoon, but do not overmix—leave some lumps in the batter. Let the batter rest for 30 minutes.

Prepare the fish   Slice the fish fillets on a bias into 8 pieces, each approximately ½ inch thick. Place in a bowl (glass, stainless steel, or ceramic) and toss in the lemon juice. Season with salt and freshly ground black pepper, and refrigerate for 15 minutes.

Remove the fish from the refrigerator and pat dry. Pour 2 inches of the oil into a deep heavy-bottomed pot. Heat the oil to 360°F to 370°F.

Season the flour with salt and freshly ground black pepper. Dredge the fish pieces in the seasoned flour and dip in the batter to coat completely. Add to the hot oil.

Cook until a dark golden color, turning once. This should take 5 to 6 minutes in total. Remove from the oil using tongs or a slotted spoon, and drain on paper towels. Immediately season with salt.

Serve with the Honey-Mustard Beer Sauce and lemon wedges on the side.

HALIBUT FILLET WITH
APPLE CIDER RELISH

Halibut is one of my favorite fishes. The mild flavor is very receptive to all kinds of preparations and balances well with many flavors. Leaving the skin on the fillets while cooking will help hold them together; just remove it before serving. Serve this with grilled apples—trim off the ends and halve the apples horizontally. Season with olive oil, salt and pepper, and chopped fresh mint before grilling until tender. Or serve with coarsely chopped radicchio and sliced fennel dressed with one part apple cider vinegar to two to three parts extra-virgin olive oil, and seasoned with salt and pepper.

SERVES 4

4 (5–6 oz) halibut fillets, skin on	1 medium-sized red apple
Juice of ½ lemon	1 Tbsp apple jelly
¼ cup wildflower honey, plus more to taste	¼ cup diced red onion
	Pinch of red chili flakes (optional)
2 Tbsp apple cider vinegar, plus more to taste	2 Tbsp sliced fresh mint
	1 Tbsp extra-virgin olive oil

Season the halibut with salt and freshly ground black pepper and coat with the lemon juice. Cover and set aside for at least 15 minutes.

Place the honey in a saucepan and heat on medium-high. Bring to a boil and cook until the honey is reduced by half and begins to caramelize and darken, swirling the pan to help color the honey evenly (this will take just a few minutes). Remove from the heat and carefully add the vinegar. Place the pan back on the heat and reduce by half again.

Peel and core the apple, and cut into ½-inch dice. Add the apple, apple jelly, onion, and chili flakes (if using) to the pan, and cook for 1 to 2 minutes to soften the mixture slightly. Transfer to a small bowl. Let cool, and then fold in the mint. Season with salt and freshly ground black pepper. Taste and add more vinegar and/or honey if you like. Set aside at room temperature.

Heat a heavy-bottomed frying pan on medium heat. Pat the fillets dry with paper towels and coat lightly with the olive oil. Place the fillets into the hot pan, and sear for 4 to 5 minutes on each side. (If you'd prefer to cook your halibut on the grill, heat a charcoal or gas grill to medium-high heat. Place the fillets on the grill, skin side down first, and cook for 4 to 5 minutes on each side. Turn the fish only once to prevent it from breaking.)

Plate and top with the relish.

 Bees do not hibernate during the winter and a hive may consume as much as 45 pounds (20 kg) of honey to make it through the season.

PAN-FRIED TROUT WITH ARUGULA, WALNUT, AND HONEY PESTO

I always associate fresh trout with spring. Trout seems to taste better early in the season when the waters are still cold. As a youngster I loved to go fishing with my friends—I couldn't wait to get home and cook what we caught, maybe with some sautéed new potatoes from my parents' garden. If we fished in the evening, then I'd be sure to have pan-fried trout with my eggs the next morning. I like to simply season trout with salt and pepper and sear it in butter and olive oil, but the arugula pesto is wonderful here too—arugula has a distinctively nutty, peppery flavor, which the honey and walnuts balance well with.

SERVES 4

4 (4–5 oz) trout fillets, skin on
2 Tbsp unsalted butter
1 Tbsp extra-virgin olive oil

PESTO

2 cups fresh arugula
½ cup Italian parsley
¼ cup chopped walnuts
1 Tbsp fresh lemon juice
1 Tbsp honey
¼ cup extra-virgin olive oil

Season the fillets with salt and freshly ground black pepper. Heat a 10-inch nonstick frying pan on medium-high heat. Add the butter and olive oil and let the foam subside. Place the fillets into the pan flesh side up and cook for 3 to 4 minutes. Turn over the fillets and cook for another 2 to 3 minutes or until the flesh just begins to flake when tested with a fork.

While the trout is cooking, process the pesto ingredients in a food processor or blender. Don't make the sauce too smooth–some texture should remain. Season with salt and freshly ground black pepper to taste.

Plate the trout, one fillet per person, and top with the pesto.

HONEY AND LEMON–BRINED
ROAST CHICKEN LEGS

This recipe can be used for chicken breasts or even whole chickens. (The brine times will vary, however; see the chart in the introduction [page 23].) But chicken legs are a more economical cut of poultry. They are also much more flavorful (in my opinion) and stay moist when roasted. Note that brining in a plastic bag minimizes the amount of brine needed.

SERVES 4

4 whole chicken legs
 (thigh and drumstick)

2 cups chilled Basic Honey Brine
 (see page 25)

4 (4-inch) sprigs fresh rosemary

1 tsp red chili flakes

1 lemon

Rinse the chicken legs under cold water and pat dry. Place into a large freezer bag, and add the brine, rosemary, and chili flakes.

With a sharp vegetable peeler, peel the rind from the lemon in several large pieces, being careful to cut off only the rind and not the white pith. Add to the bag. Cut the lemon in half and squeeze the juice into the bag.

Force out as much air as possible from the bag and seal. Place on a plate or tray and refrigerate for 4 hours, periodically turning and massaging the brine into the chicken legs through the bag to evenly distribute the flavors.

Remove the chicken from the bag and pat dry. Strain the brine through a fine-meshed sieve, discarding the liquid and reserving the rosemary, lemon rind, and chili flakes. Divide them into 4 piles on a greased or parchment paper–lined roasting pan.

Place one leg, skin side up, onto each pile. Cover and let rest for 1 hour. Preheat the oven to 325°F.

Roast for 1 hour or until a meat thermometer reads 165°F to 170°F.

CHEF'S TIP

To extract more flavor from rosemary or any fresh woody herb, cover it with the flat side of a chef's knife and tap gently with the palm of your hand or a closed fist. This releases more of the essential oils. The same can be done with lemon rind.

HONEY AND LAVENDER–BRINED CHICKEN BREAST

If you frequent farmers' markets, you may be familiar with lavender jelly. Floral and herbal jellies are often made with apples because the pectin in the apples helps to set jelly. To make a quick version, empty an 8-ounce jar of apple jelly into a small saucepan. Add just the flowers of 6 to 8 sprigs of fresh or dried lavender (the dried will result in a stronger flavor). Warm the mixture on low heat for 5 minutes. Remove from the heat and set aside for 10 minutes. Strain through a fine-meshed sieve and pour back into the cleaned jelly jar.

SERVES 4

4 (6 oz) boneless, skinless chicken breasts

1 cup chilled Basic Honey Brine (see page 25)

6 sprigs fresh or dried lavender

2 bay leaves, crushed

6 whole cloves

6 whole allspice, crushed

2 Tbsp extra-virgin olive oil

2 cups chicken stock

¼ cup lavender jelly (see headnote for a quick homemade version)

1 Tbsp cold unsalted butter

Place the chicken breasts into a large freezer bag. Add the brine along with the lavender, bay leaves, cloves, and allspice. Press out as much air as possible from the bag and seal.

Place on a plate or tray and refrigerate for 2 hours, turning the bag and massaging the chicken two or three times during the brining time to redistribute the flavors. For a more intense flavor, brine the breasts for a longer period of time.

Remove the breasts from the bag and pat dry. Discard the brine mixture. Preheat the oven to 325°F.

Add the olive oil to a frying pan on medium-high heat. Sear the chicken so it is golden brown on both sides. Transfer to a baking dish and do not clean the pan. Place the chicken in the oven for 8 to 10 minutes or until a meat thermometer reads 165°F to 170°F.

Meanwhile, place the pan on medium-high heat and add the chicken stock. Bring to a boil while scraping to incorporate the brown bits at the bottom of the pan, and reduce by half. Add the lavender jelly and reduce again to desired consistency. Remove from the heat, and whisk the butter into the sauce until melted and smooth. Serve overtop of the chicken.

 There are around 40,000 to 60,000 bees in an average beehive and only 1 queen.

PAN-ROASTED GAME HEN
WITH HONEY-BRANDY GLAZE

Cutting up a game hen and removing the bones from the serving portions makes it much easier to slice once it's cooked. The technique of rolling the meat with the skin side out helps to keep the meat moist. Alternatively, you may use boneless chicken breasts.

SERVES 8

4 whole Cornish game hens,
   about 1 lb each

¼ cup chopped fresh rosemary

¼ cup chopped fresh sage

3–4 large garlic cloves, thinly sliced

Juice of 1 lemon

¼ cup extra-virgin olive oil

¼ cup honey

3 Tbsp brandy, divided

½ cup dry white wine

¼ cup cold unsalted butter

¼ cup chopped Italian parsley

EQUIPMENT

16 lengths of kitchen string, each
   about 8 inches long

Place a hen, breast side up, on a cutting board. With a sharp boning knife, make a cut through the skin along one side of the breast bone (in the middle), cutting all the way through to the bone. Make sure to keep the skin intact.

Being careful to stay close to the bone, start to cut the breast and wing away from the carcass. Move down to the thigh and leg, and cut those away from the carcass as well. Cut around to the back, and then remove both the breast and leg completely in one piece. Repeat with the other side.

For each half, carefully cut the meat away from all sides of the thigh bone, and then remove the thigh bone by cutting at the joint, leaving the drumstick intact. Trim the wing off of the breast.

Repeat with all of the hens. Reserve the bones and wings for making stock.

One at a time, spread each half onto a cutting board with the skin side down. Season with salt and freshly ground black pepper, and the rosemary, sage, and garlic slices, and then roll up the meat to form a cylinder. Tie it up with 2 pieces of string to help keep its shape while it cooks.

Continued on page 90

Continued from page 89

Lay the hens in a flat nonreactive dish (glass, stainless steel, or ceramic), sprinkle with the lemon juice, and refrigerate until 20 to 30 minutes before cooking time.

Preheat the oven to 425°F.

Season the hens all over with the olive oil and salt and freshly ground black pepper. Heat a large heavy-bottomed ovenproof frying pan on medium-high heat, and in 2 batches sear one side of each hen half for 2 minutes, or until browned, and then sear the other side. Remove the pan from the heat, and fit all of the hens into the pan. (Or use 2 ovenproof pans if necessary.)

In a small bowl, combine the honey and 2 tablespoons of the brandy. Brush half of the mixture onto the tops of the hens. Roast for 10 minutes. Brush again with the honey-brandy mixture, and roast for another 10 minutes.

Remove the hens from the pan and keep warm. Heat the pan on medium and add the remaining brandy. Cook slightly before adding the wine. Reduce by half. Turn off the heat and whisk or swirl in the butter. Stir in the parsley and serve with the hens.

ROASTED DUCK BREAST WITH FRESH PLUM MERLOT BUTTER SAUCE

Duck breast is complemented by rich flavors; here it's the merlot, reduced stock, and dark honey. If duck is not your thing, this same method works equally well with venison or game birds such as pheasant or quail (adjust your cooking times).

SERVES 4

4 (8–10 oz) boneless duck breasts

1 Tbsp extra-virgin olive oil

3 Tbsp unsalted butter, divided

2 Tbsp minced shallots

2 cloves garlic, minced

1 cup merlot

10–12 fresh Italian prune plums, pitted and diced

1 cup chicken stock

⅓ cup dark honey such as buckwheat

Trim the duck breasts of excess fat. With a sharp knife, score the skin (and into the layer of fat underneath) in a crisscross pattern at ½-inch intervals. Salt the skin, rubbing the salt well into the scored fat.

Heat a heavy-bottomed pan on medium to medium-high heat, and add the olive oil and 1 tablespoon of the butter. As the foam from the butter subsides, add the duck breasts skin side down, and sear for 2 minutes or until browned. Sear the other side until browned.

Place skin side down in a baking pan and set aside.

Preheat the oven to 400°F.

Drain the excess fat from the pan and lower the heat to medium. Add the shallots and cook, stirring, until soft. Add the garlic and cook for 30 seconds to 1 minute, being careful not to brown the garlic. Add the merlot and reduce the mixture by half.

Add the plums and chicken stock and bring to a simmer. Cook until the plums are tender and the sauce has reduced by half, about 10 minutes. Press the mixture through a fine-meshed sieve into a clean saucepan, and add the honey. Set aside.

Continued on page 92

Continued from page 91

Roast the duck in the oven for 12 to 14 minutes, or until a meat thermometer reads 135°F to 140°F, for medium-rare. (For medium, roast until 140°F to 145°F.) Let the duck rest, covered, for 10 minutes before serving. The internal temperature will increase by approximately 5°F.

Meanwhile, bring the plum sauce to a simmer on medium heat. Whisk in the remaining 2 tablespoons of butter, season to taste with salt and freshly ground black pepper, and remove from the heat.

To serve, divide the sauce onto 4 serving plates. Slice each breast on a bias into 5 or 6 pieces and place on top of the sauce.

 It takes about 20 pounds (10 kg) of honey to produce about 2 pounds (1 kg) of bee wax.

SWEET AND FIERY
HONEY-GARLIC SPARERIBS

Tender, juicy ribs are the highlight of many a summer BBQ. These ribs are baked in the oven, but you can finish them on the outdoor grill for the last 20 minutes of cooking. Experiment with wood chips to add an extra dimension of flavor.

SERVES 4

4 lb pork spareribs (back or side)

6 cloves garlic, minced or finely grated, divided

2 Tbsp minced or finely grated fresh ginger, divided

½ tsp freshly ground black pepper

1 Tbsp sambal oelek or to taste

½ cup honey

¼ cup light soy sauce

1 Tbsp cornstarch dissolved in 1 Tbsp water

Preheat the oven to 275°F.

Rinse the spareribs and pat dry. Cut into serving-sized pieces, and place in a shallow roasting pan large enough to hold the ribs in one layer. Toss with half of the garlic and ginger.

Add ½ inch of water to the pan. Cover with foil and bake for 2 hours and 30 minutes or until tender. Increase the oven temperature to 350°F.

Drain the fat and juices that have accumulated in the baking pan into a saucepan, and bring to a boil. Reduce to about ½ cup, skimming off and discarding the fat.

Combine the pepper, sambal oelek, honey, soy sauce, and cornstarch mixture along with the remaining garlic and ginger, and add to the saucepan. Bring back to a boil and simmer for 1 minute to cook the cornstarch.

Brush the ribs liberally with the sauce and bake, uncovered, for another 20 minutes. Baste with more sauce every 5 minutes until the ribs are completely tender.

PORK TENDERLOIN
WITH SWEET ONION
AND MEAD SAUCE

Mead is a honey wine and varies greatly in style and character, anywhere from sweet and syrupy with a distinct flavor of honey (usually served as a dessert wine) to something much drier with just a subtle hint of honey. It will often have notes of herbs and fruit flavors. Any and all varieties will work well in this recipe; however, drier meads will obviously result in a sauce that is less sweet. Adjust the sweetness with a little bit of honey.

SERVES 6–8

2 (12–14 oz) pork tenderloins

½ cup Basic Honey Brine
   (see page 25)

3–4 large cloves garlic, divided

2 Tbsp extra-virgin olive oil, divided

4–5 medium-sized yellow onions

½ cup mead

¾ cup beef, chicken, or
   vegetable stock, divided

1 Tbsp cornstarch

4–6 sprigs fresh thyme

1–2 Tbsp honey (optional)

Trim the tenderloins of any excess fat, and remove the silver skin (the outer layer of connective tissue) by forcing the tip of a sharp knife under the skin, and then running the knife at a slight upward angle along the length of the silver skin. Place the tenderloins in a large freezer bag, and add the brine. Crush two of the garlic cloves and add to the bag. Press out as much air as possible from the bag and seal.

Place on a plate or tray and refrigerate for 3 hours. Remove the tenderloins from the brine and pat dry; discard the brine. Season with freshly ground black pepper.

Heat a frying pan on medium and add 1 tablespoon of the olive oil. Add the tenderloins, one at a time, and sear until browned on all sides. Remove from the pan and set aside. Do not wash the pan.

Quarter the onions and slice very thinly to yield about 4 cups. Add the remaining tablespoon of olive oil to the pan; place on medium heat and add the onions. Mince the remaining 1 or 2 cloves of garlic and add to the onions.

Season the onions lightly with salt and freshly ground black pepper. Reduce the heat to low and cook very slowly, stirring frequently, until the onions are soft and lightly colored. This may take 20 to 30 minutes or more. Add the mead and increase the heat to medium. Cook until the liquid has almost all evaporated. Add ½ cup of the stock and bring to a simmer.

Dissolve the cornstarch in the remaining ¼ cup of stock, which should be either cold or at room temperature, and stir into the onions. Add the thyme sprigs and continue to cook slowly.

Meanwhile, preheat the oven to 375°F.

Roast the tenderloins for 10 to 12 minutes or until a meat thermometer reads 145°F to 150°F. Let the tenderloins rest, covered loosely with foil, for 10 minutes.

When the onions are done, fish out the thyme from the sauce and scrape off as many leaves from the stems as you can. Add them back into the mixture. Season the onions with salt and freshly ground black pepper to taste. For a slightly sweeter sauce, add honey. If desired, purée the onions, partially or completely, using a food processor or blender.

Slice the tenderloin and serve with the onion sauce.

SLOW-ROASTED HONEY-BRINED PORK SHOULDER

In my opinion, the most flavorful cuts of pork are from the shoulder. The ratio of fat to muscle is almost perfect from a culinary point of view—25 to 30 percent fat is standard for sausage making, and that's the average for pork shoulder. Even though most of the fat gets rendered from the meat during cooking, it helps to keep the meat moist and flavorful. Look for a roast with good marbling, and ask your butcher to tie the roast if it isn't sold that way (tying helps to maintain the shape). Spices like fennel (which has forever been used to flavor pork), anise, and cumin go very well with the natural "sweetness" of pork—experiment with your own blends.

SERVES 4–6

2–2½ lb boneless pork shoulder roast, tied

6–8 large cloves garlic, crushed

1 Tbsp whole fennel seeds

2 tsp chipotle powder

1 tsp red chili flakes

1 cup Basic Honey Brine (see page 25)

1–2 Tbsp extra-virgin olive oil

3 Tbsp honey

2 cups chicken stock or vegetable stock, divided

1 Tbsp cornstarch

Place the roast in a large freezer bag, and add the garlic, fennel seeds, chipotle powder, chili flakes, and brine. Press out as much air as possible and seal the bag.

Place on a plate or tray and refrigerate for 24 hours. Periodically turn the bag and massage the pork to redistribute the flavors. After the brining time, remove the pork from the brine, reserving the brine, and pat dry.

Strain the brine through a fine-meshed sieve, discarding the liquid. Set aside the strained garlic and spices.

Preheat the oven to 300°F.

Heat a heavy-bottomed frying pan on medium to medium-high heat. Rub the roast with the olive oil, and add to the pan. Sear for 1 to 2 minutes on each side until well browned and place in a roasting pan.

Add the honey to the frying pan and bring to a boil. Stir constantly and cook the honey until it darkens—a light-colored honey should become a mahogany color.

Add 1½ cups of the stock to the frying pan, scraping any remaining bits from the bottom of the pan. Add this honey and stock mixture to the roasting pan, along with the garlic and spices from the brine.

Cover and roast the pork until a meat thermometer reads 150°F to 155°F, about 2½ to 3 hours. Uncover the roast and cook for another 30 minutes, basting with the juices every 10 minutes.

When the roast is done, remove from the roasting pan, cover loosely with foil, and set aside in a warm place to rest.

Combine the remaining stock and the cornstarch in a small bowl, and stir into the fat and juices in the roasting pan. Place on medium heat on the stovetop, and bring to a simmer. Cook until the sauce has thickened. If it's too thick, add some water. Adjust the flavor with salt and freshly ground black pepper if needed. The sauce will have a sweet edge to it; you can also add more honey if desired.

Press the sauce though a fine-meshed sieve, and serve over thin slices of the roast.

CHEF'S TIP
Chipotles are smoked jalapeños, a mild chili. Powdered chipotle adds great depth of flavor and color to a dish. Substitute smoked paprika if you prefer something milder.

GRILLED VEAL CHOPS WITH RHUBARB HONEY GLAZE

This recipe also works very well with pork loin chops or chicken breasts and with different spices or fruit—use what's in season. The chops can also be cooked on the stovetop in a cast iron skillet or ridged grill pan.

SERVES 4

4 (6–8 oz) bone-in veal rib chops	**RHUBARB HONEY GLAZE**
4–6 large sprigs fresh rosemary, roughly chopped	2 Tbsp whole fennel seeds
	1 Tbsp vegetable oil
1 tsp freshly ground black pepper	1 small white onion, diced
¼ cup dry white wine	2 Tbsp minced fresh ginger
1 Tbsp vegetable oil	2 cups diced fresh rhubarb
½ tsp table salt	¼ cup dry white wine
	1 cup wildflower honey

Rub the chops with the rosemary and pepper. Place into a shallow dish or container to fit snugly, and add the white wine, tossing to coat. Cover and refrigerate for at least 2 hours or overnight.

Make the rhubarb honey glaze Crush the fennel seeds with the back of a heavy knife. Heat a medium saucepan on medium, and add the oil. Add the onion and ginger and cook, stirring, for 30 seconds to 1 minute until fragrant. Add the fennel seeds. Stir and cook the mixture for another 2 to 3 minutes to slightly toast the fennel.

Add the rhubarb and the white wine, and lower the heat to a simmer. Cook until the rhubarb is completely soft and falling apart, about 20 minutes. If the mixture becomes dry before the rhubarb is cooked, add a few spoonfuls of water.

Remove from the heat and purée in a food processor or blender. Press through a fine-meshed sieve into a bowl, and stir in the honey while the mixture is still warm. Season with salt and freshly ground black pepper. Set aside until needed.

Grill the veal chops   Remove the chops from the marinade. Scrape off any pieces of rosemary, and pat dry. Set aside, covered, for 20 to 30 minutes at room temperature.

Heat a charcoal or gas grill to medium-high. Rub the chops with the oil and salt and grill for 4 to 5 minutes on each side for medium-rare. Spread 2 to 3 tablespoons of the rhubarb-honey mixture onto each veal chop, and cover the grill, cooking for another 5 minutes. Remove the chops from the grill.

Loosely cover the chops with foil and allow to rest for 10 minutes before serving. Serve with extra rhubarb sauce on the side.

BEEF TENDERLOIN WITH GORGONZOLA CHEESE AND HONEY PEPPER STREUSEL

Rich red meat with blue cheese has always been a popular combination. The streusel topping—a savory version of what's usually used to top muffins, pies, and fruit crumbles— adds a bit of interest and texture to the finished dish. Pair it with any roasted or grilled meat dish where you want a crispy finish.

SERVES 4

4 (5–6 oz) beef tenderloin steaks

2 Tbsp (1 fl oz) full-bodied red wine

1 Tbsp buckwheat honey

1 Tbsp extra-virgin olive oil

1 Tbsp finely chopped fresh rosemary
   or to taste

1 tsp coarse sea salt or to taste

⅓ cup Gorgonzola

HONEY PEPPER STREUSEL

7 Tbsp all-purpose flour

2 Tbsp unsalted butter, softened

2 Tbsp buckwheat honey

2 tsp whole black peppercorns,
   coarsely ground

1 tsp coarse sea salt

Place the steaks in a shallow dish or container, and add the wine, honey, olive oil, rosemary, and salt. Rub into the steaks to coat. Cover and set aside at room temperature for 30 minutes.

Make the honey pepper streusel Preheat the oven to 400°F. Add all of the ingredients to a bowl. Using your hands, combine the mixture to achieve a crumbly texture. Spread on a baking sheet, and bake for 10 minutes or until lightly browned and crisp. Cool on the baking sheet. (The streusel can be made beforehand and stored in an airtight container for up to 1 week.)

Finish the steaks Remove the steaks from the marinade and gently pat dry. Grill the steaks on medium-high or sear in a hot pan to just before the desired doneness: the internal temperature should be 120°F for rare, 130°F for medium-rare, and 140°F for medium.

If you're grilling the steaks, top with the cheese and the streusel, and cover the grill until the cheese is soft and the streusel begins to color slightly. If you're using the stovetop, place the steaks on a baking sheet and top with the cheese and streusel, and place under a preheated broiler for 30 seconds.

VARIATIONS

- Substitute tender cuts of game meat such as venison or bison.
- For the streusel, the variations are endless! Any savory ingredient can be added, such as minced garlic (raw or roasted), ground nuts, or finely chopped fresh herbs. To use as a topping for grilled or roasted fish, experiment with lighter honeys such as wildflower or acacia, and add lemon or orange zest.

SLOW-ROASTED BEEF BRISKET

We all need some comfort food every once in a while—though it may not be the best for us health-wise, it does a lot of good emotionally! This is definitely comfort food, and a perfect weekend dish for good friends and family. Serve with boiled potatoes and steamed vegetables.

SERVES 6–8

4–5 lb beef brisket

4 cups Basic Honey Brine
(see page 25)

1 medium-sized white onion,
cut into 8 wedges

2 stalks celery, cut into 4 pieces

2 medium-sized carrots, peeled
and cut into 4 pieces

¼ cup all-purpose flour

½ cup (4 fl oz) dry white wine

3 cups low-sodium beef stock or water

½ cup whole-grain mustard

EQUIPMENT
Kitchen string to tie up the brisket

Trim the beef brisket of excess pockets of fat, leaving up to ½ inch on the outer surface. Tie up the brisket in 4 to 5 places to help hold it together as it cooks. (Your butcher may do this for you.)

Put the brisket into a flat casserole dish or roasting pan large enough to hold it. Pour in the brine, cover, and refrigerate overnight.

Preheat the oven to 300°F.

Remove the brisket from the brine, discarding the brine. Rinse well and pat dry.

Place the onion, celery, and carrots into the bottom of a roasting pan that will fit the brisket snugly. Place the brisket on top of the vegetables. Add enough water that it comes 1 inch up the sides of the pan, and cover.

Roast for 2½ hours for a 4 lb roast, and 3 hours for a 5 lb roast, adding water as needed to prevent the pan from drying.

Remove the lid and continue to cook for 45 minutes to 1 hour or until tender and browned on the surface. (To keep the roast moist during this last period of cooking and to aid browning, baste every 15 minutes with juices from the pan.)

Transfer the roast to a plate, and cover loosely with foil while making the sauce. Remove the vegetables from the roasting pan and dice. Drain the excess fat from the pan, leaving about ¼ cup. Add the diced vegetables back into the pan.

Place on medium heat on the stovetop, and stir in the flour, incorporating all of the remaining fat. Brown lightly, and then add the wine and stir to combine. When the wine is almost evaporated, add the stock or water. Bring to a simmer and reduce to a desired consistency.

Press the sauce through a fine-meshed sieve into a small saucepan, and stir in the mustard. Season the sauce with salt and freshly ground pepper if necessary.

Slice the brisket, keeping the string on (this will make slicing easier), and serve family style with the sauce poured overtop.

HONEY-GLAZED FLANK STEAK

Flank steak is a cut of beef that most home cooks are unfamiliar with or shy away from, which is unfortunate as it's versatile and can be simply prepared. Flank steak is a superlean cut with a very obvious grain. (A good substitute for flank steak is skirt steak, which is similarly textured and just as flavorful.) The keys to cooking it are high heat, keeping it medium-rare or rare, and, most important, letting the meat rest for at least 10 to 15 minutes before slicing. This is a great prepare-ahead cut. For lunch, it's tasty sliced on top of a salad of mixed greens, or cooked beets and blue cheese, tossed with olive oil and balsamic. For an hors d'oeuvre, toast slices of baguette in a frying pan with olive oil, and top with slices of steak and shredded arugula.

SERVES 4–6

1 lb beef flank steak (or skirt steak)	MARINADE
1 Tbsp extra-virgin olive oil	½ cup red wine
½ tsp table salt	¼ cup buckwheat honey
1 tsp cornstarch	1 Tbsp extra-virgin olive oil
	3–4 cloves garlic, crushed
	2 Tbsp smoked paprika
	2 Tbsp finely chopped fresh thyme
	½ tsp red chili flakes
	½ tsp freshly ground black pepper

Remove any fat or sinew from the steak. In a nonreactive dish or bowl (glass, stainless steel, or ceramic), combine all of the marinade ingredients. Add the steak and cover; refrigerate for several hours or overnight.

Remove the steak from the marinade, reserving the marinade, and pat the steak dry with paper towels. Heat a heavy-bottomed frying pan or a charcoal or gas grill on high. Rub the steak with the olive oil, and season on both sides with the salt.

Place in the pan or on the grill, and sear for 4 to 5 minutes on each side until well browned. Remove from the heat, cover loosely with foil, and allow to rest for 10 minutes before slicing.

While the meat is resting, place the reserved marinade in a small saucepan. Dissolve the cornstarch in 2 tablespoons of cold water, and stir into the marinade. Heat the mixture to a simmer on medium heat, stirring until clear. Season to taste, and strain through a fine-meshed sieve. Brush onto the cooked flank steak.

To serve, slice the meat very thinly on a bias, and across the grain to ensure tenderness.

 Bees have a top flight speed of around 20 miles per hour (35 km/hr).

BRAISED BEEF SHORT RIBS
WITH BING CHERRIES
AND BALSAMIC GLAZE

Short ribs have gained popularity in recent years. It's no wonder—as with many other tough cuts, with a little time and care you can get a remarkably delicious result. After long and slow cooking, the fat and connective tissue will mostly dissolve and the meat will completely tenderize. And this cherry recipe is a special one, not just because it uses a variety of cherries grown here in British Columbia. (The other main commercial variety is Lapin; both are large, plump, and black.) You can serve it with grilled or roasted game meats, seared duck breast, or roast chicken, and—if you substitute cider vinegar and white wine for the balsamic vinegar and red wine—with lighter meats such as pork tenderloin or chicken breast. The variation listed at the end of the recipe is delicious on its own, as a wonderful breakfast. Or try it on top of vanilla ice cream, dress up a rich chocolate brownie, or do both at the same time!

SERVES 4

2 lb beef short ribs

¼ cup all-purpose flour

2 Tbsp vegetable oil

1 small onion, minced

2 cloves garlic, minced

1 cup (8 fl oz) red wine
   (I prefer merlot)

4 sprigs fresh rosemary
   or thyme or to taste

1 cup beef or chicken stock

CHERRIES IN A BALSAMIC GLAZE

1 lb fresh Bing cherries

¼ cup honey

1 cup (8 fl oz) red wine
   (I prefer merlot)

1 cinnamon stick

6 whole cloves

1 Tbsp balsamic vinegar

Pinch of table salt

Heat a large heavy-bottomed braising pot on medium. While it heats, season the short ribs with salt and freshly ground black pepper and dredge in the flour. Add the oil to the pot.

Continued on page 108

Continued from page 106

Add the short ribs without crowding the pot and brown well on all sides. You may have to do this in batches. Remove the browned ribs to a paper towel–lined plate.

Reduce the heat to low and add the onion and garlic to the pot. Brown lightly and add the wine and rosemary or thyme. Reduce by half and then add the stock. Reduce by half again and add the short ribs back to the pot.

Cover tightly with a lid or foil, and simmer on low heat for 2 hours. The ribs may also be simmered in a 300°F oven. Check the pot occasionally to ensure the liquid has not reduced too much.

Prepare the cherries   Wash and pit the cherries. In a nonreactive frying pan (not aluminum, copper, or cast iron), place the cherries, honey, and wine, and gently bring to a simmer on low heat. Simmer for 2 to 3 minutes or until the cherries are just tender and give a little resistance when poked with the tip of a knife.

Strain the cherries through a sieve or colander into a bowl; reserve the straining liquid. Quarter the cherries and set aside.

Return the straining liquid to the pan and add the cinnamon, cloves, balsamic vinegar, and salt. Bring back to a simmer on medium heat and cook until the mixture starts to become syrupy. Add the quartered cherries and reduce to a jamlike consistency.

Finish the ribs   Once the ribs are tender, add the cherry mixture to the braising pot, and remove from the heat. Preheat the oven to 300°F (or if you were simmering the ribs in the oven, keep the oven on). Spread out the ribs onto a foil-lined baking sheet, and top with any of the cherry mixture that may be left in the pot.

Roast for 30 minutes or until the mixture has formed a glaze on the ribs. Baste the ribs every 10 minutes or so until a good glaze forms.

VARIATION

For a sweeter version of the cherry sauce that's less jamlike and great for desserts, keep the cherries whole and don't add them back into the pan while the syrup reduces. Increase the amount of honey to ½ cup. Add the scraped-out tiny seeds of a vanilla bean and the split-open bean with the cinnamon and cloves (or add ½ teaspoon of vanilla extract to the cooling cherry mixture); omit the balsamic vinegar and salt. Once the syrup is reduced to about ¾ cup to 1 cup, pour it over the cherries and let it cool to room temperature. (You can also use white Rainier cherries and a fruity white wine such as Riesling or a spicy Gewürztraminer.)

DESSERTS AND SWEET TREATS

GRILLED FRESH PEACHES

This quick and tasty summertime dessert is incredibly easy, especially if you're already outdoors enjoying a casual grilled dinner. If you want to make this a little more decadent, serve with Honey Vanilla-Bean Ice Cream (page 116). And try grilling other fruit too, such as pineapples, nectarines, and pears. Freestone peaches have a stone that will easily separate if the peach is ripe.

SERVES 4–8

4 medium-sized ripe freestone peaches

½ tsp ground cinnamon

½ tsp ground ginger

¼ tsp (or a good pinch) freshly
grated nutmeg

¼ cup melted unsalted butter

2 Tbsp honey

2 Tbsp (1 fl oz) late-harvest wine or
your favorite dessert wine (optional)

Heat a gas or charcoal grill to medium-high.

Cut the peaches in half and remove the pits. Do not peel. Place the peaches in a bowl, and add the cinnamon, ginger, and nutmeg. Drizzle with the melted butter and toss gently to coat.

Place the peach halves cut side down on the grill and cook for 60 to 90 seconds or until beginning to color. Turn them over and grill for another 60 to 90 seconds.

Remove to a serving platter. While still warm, drizzle with the honey and the wine (if using).

CHERRY AND BALSAMIC VINEGAR SORBETTO

Use more or less lemon juice depending on your taste and the sweetness of the fruit. If the sorbetto is too hard, let it sit in the refrigerator for 30 minutes before serving.

MAKES ABOUT 1 QUART

1 lb fresh black cherries, unpitted (about 3 cups)

1 cup honey

¾ cup granulated sugar

2¼ cups water

Grated zest and juice of 1 small lemon (about 2 Tbsp juice)

1 Tbsp balsamic vinegar or to taste

Place the cherries, honey, sugar, and water into a saucepan, and bring to a simmer on medium heat. Cook until the cherries are soft and the sugar has dissolved.

Purée through a food mill; this will also remove the pits. Add the lemon zest, lemon juice, and balsamic vinegar.

Cool the mixture completely. Freeze in an ice-cream maker following the manufacturer's instructions.

Alternately, you can pour the mixture into a metal baking pan or bowl and place in the freezer. After about 20 minutes, when the sorbetto begins to solidify, scrape the ice from the edges and stir in. Continue to do so every 15 to 20 minutes until the sorbetto is uniformly frozen.

RHUBARB, HONEY, AND FRESH THYME SORBETTO

Sorbetto is usually served in small portions—a little goes a long way. If you want a lighter dessert, or something that cleanses the palate before dessert number two, this sorbetto is excellent. The sharp tang of fresh ginger works well with the honey here, so the result isn't overly sweet.

SERVES ABOUT 8–12

About 4 oz piece fresh ginger, unpeeled

½ lb fresh or frozen rhubarb, cubed (1½ cups)

¾ cup honey

2 cups water

2 Tbsp chopped fresh thyme

2 Tbsp fresh lemon juice, more if needed

¼ cup (2 fl oz) dry white wine

Make ginger juice by processing the ginger with 2 to 3 tablespoons of water in a food processor until very fine. Line a fine-meshed sieve with cheesecloth and squeeze the juice into a small bowl. Measure out 1 tablespoon (or according to taste).

In a saucepan on medium heat, combine the rhubarb, honey, and water. Cook until the rhubarb is tender, about 8 to 10 minutes. Cool slightly and purée in a blender or food processor. Pour into a bowl and add the ginger juice, thyme, lemon juice, and wine. If it's too sweet, adjust with more lemon juice.

Cool the mixture completely, and freeze in an ice-cream maker following the manufacturer's instructions.

Alternately, you can pour the mixture into a metal baking pan or bowl and place in the freezer. After about 20 minutes, when the sorbetto begins to solidify, scrape the ice from the edges and stir in. Continue to do so every 15 to 20 minutes until the sorbetto is uniformly frozen.

HONEY VANILLA-BEAN ICE CREAM

The world's most popular ice cream flavor gets a rich boost of flavor—honey!

MAKES 1 QUART

1¾ cups whole milk

2 cups heavy cream (35%)

1 vanilla bean or 2 tsp vanilla extract

8 large egg yolks

⅔ cup honey

Place the milk and cream in a heavy-bottomed pot.

Split the vanilla bean (if using) lengthwise with a sharp knife, scrape out the tiny seeds with the back of a knife, and add the seeds and the split-open vanilla bean to the pot. Bring the contents to a simmer on medium heat.

Combine the egg yolks and honey in a heatproof bowl and beat until light and fluffy.

Remove the pot from the heat. Remove the vanilla bean, scraping out any seeds still attached to the bean and adding them back to the cream.

Slowly pour the hot cream into the egg yolks while whisking constantly, speeding up the pouring when about half of the cream has been added.

Cook over a pot of simmering water, stirring constantly until the mixture coats the bottom of a wooden spoon or the temperature reaches 170°F to 175°F. This may take up to 10 minutes.

Remove from the heat and continue stirring for 1 to 2 minutes to prevent overheating. Stir in the vanilla extract (if using). Strain the mixture through a fine-meshed sieve into a clean bowl. Let the mixture cool completely by placing the bowl over an ice bath and stirring, and then chill for several hours or overnight.

Freeze in an ice-cream maker following the manufacturer's instructions.

OLIVE OIL AND HONEY ICE CREAM

This is lovely served with a pinch of sea salt on top.

MAKES 1 QUART

1¼ cups whole milk	6 large egg yolks
⅓ cup honey	1¼ cups heavy cream (35%)
Pinch of salt	½ cup fruity extra-virgin olive oil

Stir the milk, honey, and salt in a heavy-bottomed saucepan on medium heat until the honey and salt are dissolved and the milk is warm.

In a heatproof bowl, whisk the egg yolks. Gradually pour the warmed milk into the egg yolks, whisking constantly. When all of the milk has been added, pour the mixture back into the pan.

Cook over a pot of simmering water while stirring constantly, until the mixture coats the back of a wooden spoon or reaches 170°F to 175°F.

Strain the mixture through a fine-meshed sieve into a clean bowl. Add the cream and whisk to combine. Add the olive oil and continue to whisk to combine.

Place the bowl over an ice bath and stir until completely cooled. Place in the refrigerator for 3 to 4 hours or overnight. Freeze in an ice-cream maker following the manufacturer's instructions.

 Bees have been in existence for around 30 million years, and humans have been cultivating their honey for millennia. Honey was even found in the ancient tombs in Egypt, and it was still edible!

EASY LEMON AND
HONEY PARFAIT

The term *parfait* usually refers to a dessert that is layered in a tall glass, most often consisting of preserved fruit (and fruit syrup), chocolate syrup, and whipped cream. This version is something quite different; it is basically an easy version of ice cream—or a frozen mousse. The whipped cream is folded into the custard, which you then freeze and don't churn. The parfait is either frozen in molds or served like ice cream.

SERVES 8

1¾ cups heavy cream (35%)

½ cup honey, divided

4 large egg yolks

2 Tbsp minced candied lemon peel

1 Tbsp minced candied ginger

In a mixing bowl, combine the cream with 2 tablespoons of the honey. Whip the cream until soft peaks form (almost firm but still slightly runny).

Combine the remaining honey with the egg yolks in a heatproof bowl, and whisk over a pot of simmering water until light yellow and thickened. Stir in the candied lemon and ginger.

Mix in approximately one-third of the whipped cream, and then carefully fold in the rest with a rubber spatula until just combined.

Pour the mixture into a freezerproof bowl or covered container, or a large mold or individual molds, and freeze. Before serving, place the parfait in the refrigerator for 20 minutes to soften slightly.

WHITE CHOCOLATE
AND HONEY MOUSSE

A quick and simple dessert when you're in a pinch. Serve with fresh berries, peaches, or figs when they're in season and a crisp cookie.

SERVES 2–4

2 oz white chocolate, coarsely chopped	2 Tbsp wildflower honey
	¾ cup heavy cream (35%)

Melt the white chocolate and honey in a double boiler or a bowl set over a pot of simmering water. As the white chocolate melts, stir occasionally to avoid overheating, and until it's smooth and free of lumps. Let cool to room temperature.

Whip the cream using an electric mixer or by hand until slightly thicker than sour cream. Whisk one-third of the whipped cream into the room-temperature white chocolate, and then carefully fold in the rest using a rubber spatula.

Portion the mixture into individual serving cups or leave the mixture in the bowl (if you'll be spooning the mousse onto serving plates). Refrigerate until firm.

SPICED HONEY AND ROASTED-YAM MOUSSE

Not as unusual as it may sound! Vegetables often show up in sweet concoctions. This is a delicious dairy-free dessert, but for a richer, more familiar "mousse" texture, fold in some whipped cream.

SERVES 6–8

1 medium-sized yam (or sweet potato)

4 large eggs, separated

¾ cup honey

1 tsp ground cinnamon

½ tsp ground ginger

¼ tsp ground nutmeg

¼ tsp ground allspice

Pinch of salt

½ cup heavy cream (35%), whipped
   to soft peaks (optional)

GARNISH

1 Tbsp light-colored honey

¼ cup toasted sliced almonds

Pinch each of ground cinnamon,
   ginger, and nutmeg

Preheat the oven to 375°F.

Scrub the yam or sweet potato, and poke it with a fork several times. Roast on a baking sheet until completely tender, about 1 hour. Slice it in half when cool enough to handle. Scoop out the flesh and put it in a food processor, discarding the skin. Process until smooth. For an even smoother consistency, press the purée through a fine-meshed sieve.

Combine the egg whites and honey in a bowl set over a pot of simmering water. Cook, stirring constantly, until the mixture reaches 160°F. Remove from the heat. Beat the whites using an electric mixer on high speed until glossy peaks form.

In a medium saucepan, combine the egg yolks, yam purée, cinnamon, ginger, nutmeg, allspice, and salt. Cook on medium heat, stirring constantly, until the mixture comes to a boil. Remove from the heat and set aside to cool.

Continued on page 122

Continued from page 121

Gently stir in one-third of the egg whites, and then gradually fold in the rest, along with the whipped cream (if using). Portion the mixture into 6 to 8 serving glasses, cover, and chill.

Make the garnish Have ready two 12- × 12-inch pieces of parchment paper. In a small saucepan on medium, heat the honey. Cook until it begins to caramelize or until darkened. This will take a few minutes. Once the honey is evenly colored, remove from the heat and stir in the almonds and the spices.

Spread the warm mixture onto one of the pieces of parchment. Top with the second piece of parchment, and roll flat with a rolling pin as thin as possible. Cool until the mixture hardens, and score or break into pieces of desired size for garnishing.

GALAKTOBOUREKO

The name of this popular Greek dessert translates to "milk pie," which doesn't quite do it justice. Layers of phyllo pastry encase a delicious rich custard, all soaked in a lemon-flavored honey syrup that's commonly used in Greek desserts.

MAKES ONE 9- × 9-INCH GALAKTOBOUREKO; SERVES 16

5¾ cups milk

1 cup semolina

1¼ cups honey

2 Tbsp all-purpose flour

4 large egg yolks

Grated zest of 1 lemon

1½ tsp vanilla extract

12 sheets phyllo

½ cup melted unsalted butter

SYRUP

1 cup honey

1 cup water

Zest from 1 lemon, cut into strips

½ tsp vanilla extract

Preheat the oven to 375°F.

In a saucepan, combine the milk, semolina, honey, flour, egg yolks, and lemon zest. Bring to a simmer on medium heat and cook, stirring, until the mixture thickens, up to 10 minutes. Remove from the heat, stir in the vanilla extract, and set aside.

Line a 9- × 9-inch baking pan with parchment paper. Working quickly, line with one phyllo sheet, with the excess hanging down the sides, and brush with the melted butter. Repeat with 5 more sheets.

Pour in the custard and layer the rest of the phyllo on top, brushing more butter between the layers. Fold the overhanging edges overtop to seal. Bake for 40 minutes or until golden.

While the galaktoboureko is baking, make the syrup. Bring the honey, water, and lemon zest to a boil. Simmer for 5 minutes and set aside. When the mixture has cooled, remove the lemon zest and stir in the vanilla extract.

When the galaktoboureko is done, score the top into 16 squares or diamonds. Cool partially and pour the syrup overtop. When completely cooled, finish cutting all the way through and serve.

CHESTNUT PANNA COTTA WITH SOUR-CHERRY GRAPPA SAUCE

Panna cotta, literally "cooked cream" in Italian, is a very simple, rich dessert. Caramel, chocolate, and berry are the most popular flavors in Italy, but almost anything goes these days. If possible use a dark honey such as chestnut or buckwheat.

SERVES 8

2 tsp unflavored gelatin powder

2 cups heavy cream (35%)

¼ cup granulated sugar

2 Tbsp honey

1 vanilla bean, split open lengthwise

½ cup minced preserved chestnuts

¼ cup toasted pine nuts, to serve

SOUR-CHERRY SAUCE

2 cups preserved sour cherries in light syrup

¼ cup granulated sugar

1 Tbsp cornstarch

2 Tbsp (1 fl oz) grappa (or schnapps)

In a small bowl, sprinkle the gelatin over 2 teaspoons of cold water, and allow to soften for 5 minutes. Place the bowl over a small saucepan of simmering water to dissolve.

Combine the cream, sugar, honey, and vanilla bean in a pot and bring to a simmer on medium heat. Stir occasionally to help dissolve the sugar, and then remove from the heat and set aside for 5 minutes to steep the vanilla bean. Remove the vanilla bean, and using the back of a knife, scrape the seeds into the pot.

Stir in the dissolved gelatin and the chestnuts. Pour into eight 3-ounce (about ⅓ cup) ramekins, making sure each serving has an equal amount of chestnuts. Refrigerate for at least 6 hours or preferably overnight.

Make the cherry sauce   Drain the cherries and reserve the syrup—you should have about 1 cup of syrup. Whisk the syrup, sugar, and cornstarch together in a small saucepan, and bring to a simmer on medium heat, stirring frequently. Cook for 1 minute, and then add the cherries. Stir gently to combine and cook for 30 seconds more.

Remove from the heat and stir in the grappa. Set aside to cool.

To serve   Dip the ramekins one at a time in hot water to loosen the panna cotta. Carefully turn out onto serving plates. Top with the cherry sauce. Sprinkle with a few pine nuts and serve.

HONEY WHITE-CHOCOLATE CRÈME BRÛLÉE

Crème brûlée translates to "burnt cream," referring to the distinctive sugar layer that tops the baked custards prior to serving. Burning your dessert has never tasted so good! Of course you can also use dark chocolate (or milk chocolate) here.

SERVES 4

1 cup heavy cream (35%)

1 vanilla bean or ½ tsp vanilla extract

1 oz white chocolate, coarsely chopped, or 2–3 Tbsp white chocolate chips

3 large egg yolks

¼ cup honey

4 Tbsp granulated sugar, divided

EQUIPMENT

Butane torch (or use the oven broiler)

Preheat the oven to 300°F.

Place four 3-ounce (about ⅓ cup) ramekins into a baking pan and set aside.

Pour the cream into a small saucepan. Split the vanilla bean (if using) lengthwise with a sharp knife, scrape out the tiny seeds with the back of a knife, and add the seeds along with the split-open bean to the saucepan.

On medium-low to medium heat bring the cream to a simmer. Remove from the heat. Stir in the white chocolate, continuing to stir until the chocolate is completely melted. Stir in the vanilla extract (if using) and set the mixture aside for 5 minutes.

Place the egg yolks and honey into a bowl and combine well. Slowly pour approximately one-quarter of the cream mixture into the bowl while stirring constantly. Gradually incorporate the rest of the cream mixture, stirring constantly. Strain through a fine-meshed sieve (discard the vanilla bean and seeds).

Divide among the 4 ramekins. Pour enough boiling water into the baking pan to reach two-thirds of the way up the sides of the ramekins.

Bake for approximately 20 to 25 minutes or until the mixture has set but is still soft.

Remove the ramekins from the pan, and let it cool to room temperature. Cover and refrigerate until thoroughly chilled.

To serve, sprinkle 1 tablespoon of sugar over each custard. Light the butane torch and move the flame from side to side over the sugar, to evenly caramelize the sugar. If you don't have a torch, caramelize the sugar under the oven broiler, and let the ramekins cool before serving.

 The queen may lay up to 2,000 eggs per day in the summer when many bees are required for pollen and nectar collection.

HONEY ALMOND BRIOCHE

Brioche is a bread of French origin highly enriched with butter and eggs (and occasionally sugar, depending on it's use), which results in a light, airy texture. This version makes a wonderful pastry for breakfast or afternoon tea. This dough may also be baked in a greased and floured 9- x 5- x 3-inch loaf pan. It makes a great French toast.

MAKES 24 PORTIONS

DOUGH

⅓ cup honey

¼ cup milk

4 large eggs

1 tsp table salt

1½ cups bread flour, more if needed

1½ cups cake or pastry flour

2 Tbsp instant yeast

½ cup unsalted butter, softened

HONEY PASTRY CREAM

2¼ cups milk, divided

¼ cup plus 2 Tbsp honey, divided

½ cup cornstarch

2 large egg yolks

½ tsp vanilla extract

TOPPING

½ cup granulated sugar

½ cup honey

½ cup unsalted butter

1 cup blanched sliced almonds

Make the dough In the bowl of a stand mixer fitted with a dough hook, mix together the honey, milk, eggs, and salt. (Or use a large bowl and whisk by hand.) In a separate bowl, combine the bread flour and the cake or pastry flour with the yeast. Add the flour to the mixing bowl and mix on low (or use a wooden spoon). Gradually add the butter in small pieces.

Continue mixing until the dough forms a ball and does not stick to the sides of the bowl, about 6 to 8 minutes. You may also turn out the dough onto a floured surface and knead by hand. Add up to ½ cup bread flour as necessary. The dough should have a slightly shiny appearance and not be sticky.

Transfer the dough to a greased bowl large enough to allow the dough to double in size. Cover and refrigerate for 5 to 6 hours. (See Chef's Tip.)

Make the honey pastry cream Add 2 cups of the milk and ¼ cup of the honey to a small saucepan. Bring to a simmer on medium heat.

In a small bowl, combine the remaining ¼ cup of milk and 2 tablespoons of honey, along with the cornstarch and egg yolks, and whisk until smooth. Add the mixture to the simmering milk, and stir constantly until it comes to a simmer again. Cook for 2 minutes or until thickened, and then remove from the heat.

Press through a fine-meshed sieve into a clean bowl, and stir in the vanilla extract. Cover with plastic wrap, pressing the wrap directly onto the surface of the cream to prevent a skin from forming. Cool completely before using.

Form the brioche Coat the inside of a 13- × 9-inch cake pan with nonstick cooking spray or line with parchment paper. Punch down the dough, and spread it evenly in the prepared pan. Cover with a damp cloth, and set aside while you prepare the topping.

Combine the sugar, honey, and butter in a heatproof bowl and place over a pot of simmering water, stirring to combine. When the butter is melted, add the almonds. Remove from the heat.

Spread the topping overtop of the dough. Cover and set aside in a warm spot to rise until doubled in size.

Preheat the oven to 350°F.

Bake the brioche for 25 to 30 minutes or until lightly brown and firm when pressed in the center. Cool completely in the pan.

Slice the brioche horizontally into 2 equal layers. Spread the prepared pastry cream in between the layers. Cut into 24 portions and serve.

CHEF'S TIP

Shape the dough as soon as it has doubled in size. The high yeast content may give the dough a sour flavor if left to rise too long. You can also freeze the dough.

CHERRY HAZELNUT TIRAMISU

This is a nice summer twist on the classic Italian dessert. Tiramisu, which translated means "pick-me-up," is traditionally made with coffee, cocoa, and various liqueurs. Though there is no coffee in this recipe, it's just as good. And it's firm enough that you can serve it in slices.

SERVES 8–10

HONEY SYRUP
1 cup water
⅓ cup honey
2 Tbsp (1 fl oz) hazelnut liqueur

ZABAGLIONE FILLING
4 large egg yolks
¼ cup honey
2 Tbsp (1 fl oz) hazelnut liqueur
1 lb mascarpone cheese
¼ cup heavy cream (35%)

1 cup pitted and chopped
   fresh cherries
¼ cup chopped toasted hazelnuts
   (skins removed; see Chef's Tip)

FOR THE TIRAMISU
Savoiardi biscuits or ladyfingers
   (about 24)
¼ cup chopped toasted hazelnuts
   (skins removed; see Chef's Tip)
Powdered sugar, for dusting

Make the honey syrup   Combine the water and honey in a small saucepan and warm on low heat to combine. Stir in the hazelnut liqueur and set aside.

Make the zabaglione filling   Place the egg yolks and honey in a heatproof bowl, and whisk by hand for 1 to 2 minutes until pale and airy.

Place the bowl over a pot of simmering water, and continue to whisk until thickened and the mixture falls in an unbroken ribbon when lifted from the bowl. Add the hazelnut liqueur and continue whisking for 1 to 2 minutes. Remove from the heat and let cool slightly.

In a large bowl, briefly beat the mascarpone with a spatula or wooden spoon to soften. In a third bowl, whip the cream to soft peaks.

Fold the egg-yolk mixture into the mascarpone. Fold in the cherries and hazelnuts, and then the whipped cream, and set aside.

Assemble the tiramisu Line an 8- × 8-inch pan with plastic wrap. Evenly spread one-third of the filling in the pan. One at a time, briefly soak a third of the biscuits or ladyfingers in the syrup, and place them over the filling. Spread another third of the filling over the layer of biscuits. Continue with another layer of syrup-soaked biscuits and filling. Finally end with the last of the biscuits (also soaked in syrup) to form 3 layers each of filling and biscuits.

Cover with plastic wrap and refrigerate for 4 hours or overnight.

To serve, remove the plastic wrap from the top and turn out the tiramisu upside down onto a cutting board. Remove the rest of the plastic wrap. Top with the hazelnuts. Dust liberally with the powdered sugar. Portion into 8 to 10 pieces and serve.

CHEF'S TIP

To toast and remove the skins from hazelnuts, preheat the oven to 350°F. Spread the hazelnuts onto an ungreased baking sheet, and bake for approximately 10 minutes. Place the nuts into a clean kitchen towel, and rub off as much of the skin as you can.

MINI BLACKBERRY
GOAT-CHEESE CHEESECAKES

These little cheesecakes are perfect when something a bit sweet is desired. In place of the blackberries, raspberries and loganberries (if you can find them) are also nice, as well as fresh peaches—just dice and toss peeled peaches with a little lemon juice. Although ring molds make the baking and removal of the cheesecakes much easier, these treats can also be made in muffin pans or individual tart tins. Just be sure to grease them well to help ease removal.

MAKES 8 MINI CHEESECAKES

½ cup ground blanched almonds

2 Tbsp all-purpose flour

2 Tbsp granulated sugar

1 Tbsp unsalted butter, softened

¾ cup (6 oz) plain soft goat cheese

3 Tbsp honey, divided

1 tsp grated lemon zest

1 large egg

About 1 cup fresh blackberries,
   plus more to serve

EQUIPMENT
8 metal ring molds

Preheat the oven to 275°F.

Grease the insides of the ring molds with vegetable oil, butter, or nonstick cooking spray. Place them on a parchment paper–lined baking tray.

Blend together the almonds, flour, sugar, and butter. Divide the mixture into the molds and press to firm.

Cream together the goat cheese, 2 tablespoons of the honey, and the lemon zest. Add the egg and mix just to combine. Fill the molds with half of the cheese mixture. Divide the berries into the molds and top with the remaining goat-cheese mixture.

Bake for 20 to 25 minutes or until the tops are just firm. Let them cool to room temperature, and carefully remove from the ring molds.

To serve, drizzle with the remaining honey and top with a few fresh berries.

CHOCOLATE HONEY NUT CAKE

This is not really a cake but more of a dense chocolate-nut loaf. Serve small portions with good strong coffee. If you want to serve this as a dessert combo, pair it with something a little tart to balance the sweet richness of the cake. Lemon Cream (page 142) would also be a nice accompaniment.

MAKES 1 SMALL LOAF

5 oz extra-dark semisweet or bittersweet chocolate (at least 85% cocoa), coarsely chopped

6 Tbsp unsalted butter

2 Tbsp honey

¼ cup chopped walnuts

¼ cup chopped pistachios

¼ cup chopped toasted hazelnuts (skins removed; see Chef's Tip on page 131)

¼ cup chopped dried figs

1 Tbsp (½ fl oz) dark rum

Combine the chocolate, butter, and honey in a double boiler or a bowl set over a pot of simmering water. Stir occasionally to combine as it melts.

In a separate bowl, combine the three kinds of nuts with the figs and rum and set aside. When the chocolate melts, remove from the heat and stir in the nuts and figs.

Line a mini loaf pan or mold, approximately 3 by 5 inches, with a piece of plastic wrap large enough that it will hang down the sides, and pour in the mixture. Smooth the top and cover with the excess plastic wrap. Refrigerate until firm.

To serve, remove from the mold and cut portions using a hot moistened knife.

CHEF'S TIP

If you don't have a mini loaf pan or mold, you can also roll the mixture into a log. Just let the mixture cool for a few minutes while turning it over with a rubber spatula until it starts to set. Scrape out the mixture onto a square of parchment paper, and roll into a log. Twist the ends of the parchment tightly before refrigerating.

PANGIALLO

This sweet, very dense loaf is an Italian Christmas specialty, which as far as I know is unique to my parents' hometown of Carpineto Romano. All of my aunts would make this recipe come December, each with her own slight variation, and would give the mini loaves to lucky visitors. Serve sliced as part of an assortment of cookies and sweets. The flour in the recipe is used to keep the mixture from sticking to your hands and counter when forming the loaves.

MAKES 12 MINI LOAVES

2 lb shelled hazelnuts (skins left on or removed)

2 lb shelled walnuts

1¾ cups (½ lb) shelled Brazil nuts

¾ cup dried apricots or prunes

1⅓ cups (½ lb) raisins

3 oz semisweet or bittersweet chocolate, coarsely chopped

6 Tbsp cocoa powder

3 cups honey

About 2 cups whole wheat flour

Coarsely chop the three kinds of nuts, and place them in a very large bowl. Finely chop the dried apricots or prunes, and add them along with the raisins to the bowl.

Melt the chocolate in a double boiler or a bowl set over a pot of simmering water. Add the melted chocolate and the cocoa powder and honey to the nut mixture, and mix well.

Preheat the oven to 350°F. Grease and flour a baking sheet.

Turn out the mixture onto a work surface dusted with some of the whole wheat flour. With floured hands, shape the mixture into approximately twelve 8-inch-long loaves that are firm and compact.

Place on the prepared baking sheet and bake for 20 to 25 minutes.

Cool on a wire rack. Wrap the loaves individually in foil or plastic wrap. Although they may dry out a bit, the loaves will keep for up to 1 month.

PANFORTE

Panforte, literally "strong bread," is a famous cake from Siena in Tuscany, dating back to the 12th century. Originally a Christmas confection, it is now enjoyed year-round. Although not difficult to make, it does require some care in the preparation, especially when cooking the honey and sugar. The cake has a chewy, almost candylike texture and should be served in thin slices. Well-wrapped, the cake will keep in the refrigerator for several weeks or frozen for up to six months.

MAKES ONE 8-INCH-ROUND PANFORTE

¾ cup whole hazelnuts

¾ cup sliced blanched almonds

⅓ cup diced candied orange peel

⅓ cup diced candied lemon peel

⅓ cup diced candied citron
  (see Chef's Tip)

1 tsp grated orange zest

1 tsp grated lemon zest

½ tsp ground cinnamon

½ tsp ground cloves

½ tsp freshly ground black pepper

¼ tsp ground nutmeg

¼ tsp ground coriander

⅓ cup all-purpose flour

½ cup granulated sugar

½ cup dark honey such as buckwheat

Icing sugar, for dusting

Preheat the oven to 350°F.

Spread the hazelnuts and almonds onto an ungreased baking sheet, and bake for approximately 10 minutes or until the almonds are lightly browned.

Reduce the oven temperature to 325°F.

Use a clean kitchen towel to rub off as much of the skin from the hazelnuts as possible. Coarsely chop the hazelnuts and almonds. In a bowl, combine the nuts with the rest of the ingredients except for the granulated sugar, honey, and icing sugar.

Grease an 8-inch springform pan. Line the bottom and sides with parchment paper and lightly grease the parchment. Set aside.

Combine the sugar and honey in a medium heavy-bottomed saucepan and bring to a simmer on medium heat. Cook until a candy thermometer reads 265°F or for 3 to 4 minutes, until the mixture reaches what is referred to as the soft-ball stage. To test the mixture, drop ½ teaspoon into some cold water. If the mixture forms a firm, pliable ball between your fingers, it is ready.

Quickly add the nut mixture, and stir to combine. Scrape into the prepared pan and spread evenly using moistened hands or a spatula.

Bake until lightly browned and the edges are firm, about 40 to 50 minutes.

Cool on a wire rack until the center is firm, and then remove the sides of the pan. Cool the panforte completely. Invert it onto another wire rack. Peel off the parchment and dust well with icing sugar. To store, wrap well in plastic wrap and foil.

CHEF'S TIP

You can find candied citron at bakery supply shops. Or simply substitute extra candied lemon peel.

BITTER CHOCOLATE, CHESTNUT HONEY, AND CHERRY PIZZA

This recipe was created during one of my visits to the city of Lucca in Tuscany. I was fortunate to be invited to appear as a guest chef at Selva, a beautifully restored 15th-century villa that's part of a thousand-acre estate. A specialty of the estate is chestnut honey. Part of our culinary week included a casual pizza night. Cherries were in season, the honey was newly harvested, and I wanted to end the night on a sweet note. This is the result. Try baking the pizza on a pizza stone for a crisp crust.

MAKES ONE 10-INCH PIZZA

½ lb prepared pizza dough (see page 45)

All-purpose flour, for rolling out the dough

½ lb fresh cherries, pitted

4 oz 80%–90% chocolate bar (not baking chocolate), broken into bite-sized pieces (see Chef's Tips)

¼ cup chestnut honey or your favorite dark honey (see Chef's Tips)

Extra-virgin olive oil

Preheat the oven to 475°F. If you have a pizza stone, place it in the oven as it preheats, for 20 to 30 minutes.

Using just a small amount of flour on the work surface to prevent the dough from sticking, roll out the dough to a 10-inch circle.

Place on a pizza pan that has been coated with olive oil. (If you're using a pizza stone, place the dough on a lightly floured pizza peel or turned-over baking sheet to help slide the pizza onto the stone.)

Distribute the cherries and chocolate pieces onto the dough. Drizzle with the honey and bake for 8 to 10 minutes or until crisp.

CHEF'S TIPS

· The percentages you sometimes see on chocolate-bar labels and the labels of baking chocolate refer to the cocoa content. The higher the percentage, the more chocolaty the flavor and the less sugar was used in the production process. I use a chocolate bar for this recipe as they're thin and will melt quickly.

· Choose a full-flavored honey with an almost savory finish. Buckwheat honey would also be great here.

MELATI

Melati comes from the word *miele* ("honey"). They are similar to doughnuts. The dough should be a little firmer than bread dough. Balls of dough are formed with a spoon, fried, and then dipped in warm honey (or rolled in sugar when honey isn't available). These are usually eaten at Carnevale, a festival celebrated in Italy (and many other places around the world) 40 days before Easter.

MAKES ABOUT 30 MELATI

3 large eggs

½ cup extra-virgin olive oil

¼ cup granulated sugar

1 cup (8 fl oz) white wine

Grated zest of 1 lemon

3 cups all-purpose flour, more if needed

2 tsp baking powder

¼ tsp table salt

Vegetable oil, for deep-frying

About 1½ cups honey, for dipping

In a bowl, whisk the eggs, olive oil, and sugar until the mixture is pale yellow and doubled in volume. Beat in the white wine and lemon zest.

In another bowl, sift together the flour, baking powder, and salt. Using a rubber spatula, fold the flour into the eggs to form a soft uniform dough that will hold its shape when deep-fried.

Pour the oil into a heavy-bottomed pot to about 2 inches deep, and heat to between 360°F and 375°F. Place the honey into a heatproof bowl and warm over a pot of hot water kept on low heat.

Test the consistency of the batter by first frying one melati. Dip a soupspoon in water, and form a ball of dough about the size of a walnut. (Or use a medium-sized ice cream scoop.) Carefully drop the dough into the hot oil using a second spoon to release the dough. If the batter is not firm enough, stir in sifted flour, 1 to 2 tablespoons at a time.

Once you have the right consistency, fry the rest of the dough without overcrowding the pan. When the balls are golden brown, remove from the oil and drain on paper towels.

Dip the warm melati in the honey, and then stack onto a plate. These are best enjoyed warm.

HONEY GINGERSNAPS
WITH LEMON CREAM

These crisp, spiced treats can be formed into tubes or cups. Or just serve flat cookies with ice cream, mousse, or other desserts. As for the lemon-cream filling, it can also be used to fill crepes or prebaked tart shells. Or serve it on its own! Unfilled gingersnaps can be stored in an airtight container for 2 to 3 days.

MAKES THIRTY 3-INCH GINGERSNAPS

LEMON CREAM
Grated zest of 1 lemon
Juice of 2 lemons
2 large egg yolks
¼ cup honey
1¼ cups heavy cream (35%)

GINGERSNAPS
½ cup unsalted butter, softened
¾ cup honey

⅔ cup granulated sugar
1 cup all-purpose flour
½ tsp ground ginger
¼ tsp ground allspice
1 Tbsp brandy

EQUIPMENT
Wooden dowel or metal cannoli mold
Pastry bag

Make the lemon cream   Combine the lemon zest, lemon juice, egg yolks, and honey in a double boiler or a heatproof bowl set over a pot of simmering water. Cook, stirring constantly, until thickened and pale.

Remove from the heat and place over a bowl of ice. Stir until cooled to room temperature.

In a bowl, whip the cream until soft peaks form (almost firm but still slightly runny). Stir one-third of the whipped cream into the cooled lemon mixture, and then carefully fold in the rest. Refrigerate for 1 hour to firm it up slightly.

Make the gingersnaps   Combine all of the ingredients in the bowl of a stand mixer, and using the paddle attachment, beat the mixture until smooth. Or combine the ingredients using an electric mixer. Refrigerate for 1 hour or more until firm.

Preheat the oven to 350°F.

Form the dough into approximately 1-inch balls, and place on parchment paper–lined or nonstick baking pans, spacing the balls 4 to 5 inches apart to allow for spreading. Flatten the balls slightly with the palm of your hand.

Bake for 10 to 12 minutes, or until the cookies are uniformly colored and lacy in texture. Cool slightly on the baking sheets so you can handle the cookies, but they should still be very pliable. To make tubes, carefully lift one edge of each cookie using a spatula, and roll the gingersnap around a wooden dowel or metal cannoli mold. Allow to cool until hard and carefully remove. If the gingersnaps cool too quickly before you can shape them, place them back into the oven to warm again and make them pliable.

Using a pastry bag, fill the cookies with the Lemon Cream.

CHEF'S TIP

To make flat cookies, just leave to cool on the baking sheets for 2 to 3 minutes until firm, and then transfer to a wire rack. To make a cup shape, mold the cookie on an overturned coffee cup, drinking glass, or ramekin—any size will do. Make them quickly, about 2 to 3 at a time, so that they do not cool too fast. Wait until the gingersnaps harden before carefully removing from the mold.

HAZELNUT SUGAR COOKIES

These tender cookies are similar in texture to shortbread. The dough is very versatile, open to many uses and many variations. Use other nuts, and/or add baking spices or cocoa. You can also form the dough into a sweet tart shell or a cheesecake bottom. Just line the bottom of a tart or springform pan that you've greased and dusted with flour. Poke several times with a fork, and bake at 350°F until firm and lightly browned. Let cool before adding the tart or cheesecake filling.

MAKES ABOUT 40 COOKIES

½ cup unsalted butter, softened

¼ cup granulated sugar,
   plus more to top

2 Tbsp honey

2 large eggs

2 cups all-purpose flour,
   more if needed

1 Tbsp baking powder

½ cup finely ground toasted hazelnuts
   (skins removed; see Chef's Tip on
   page 131)

EQUIPMENT
2-inch-round cookie cutter

Cream together the butter and sugar in a bowl. Add the honey. Beat in the eggs one at a time, scraping down the sides to combine thoroughly.

Sift together the flour and baking powder into a separate bowl, and add the hazelnuts. Add this flour mixture to the butter mixture and stir or fold in until just combined. Turn out onto a lightly floured work surface, and knead very briefly.

Gather the dough into a ball and flatten slightly. Wrap in plastic wrap and chill for 30 minutes.

Preheat the oven to 350°F.

On a work surface lightly floured to prevent the dough from sticking, roll out the dough to ⅜ inch thick, using more flour if necessary.

Cut out cookies using a 2-inch-round cookie cutter, and lay them on a parchment paper–lined baking sheet. Carefully gather and roll out the dough scraps and cut out more cookies (see Chef's Tip). Brush the cookies lightly with water, and then sprinkle with sugar.

Bake for 8 to 10 minutes or until firm and slightly colored. Transfer to a wire rack to cool.

CHEF'S TIP

When rolling out dough scraps, layer them rather than gathering them all into a ball. This prevents the cookies from becoming tough.

HONEY WALNUT BARS

This is a variation on the classic German Christmas cookie *Lebkuchen*.

MAKES ONE 8- × 8-INCH PAN

⅔ cup honey

¼ cup plus 2 Tbsp granulated sugar

2 Tbsp unsalted butter

½ cup plus ¾–1 cup all-purpose flour

½ tsp baking powder

¼ tsp baking soda

½ cup chopped walnuts

2 tsp grated orange zest

¼ cup chopped candied lemon

¼ cup chopped candied ginger

¼ tsp ground cardamom

1 tsp ground cinnamon

Pinch of ground cloves

HONEY LEMON GLAZE

2 Tbsp granulated sugar

¼ cup honey

2 tsp grated lemon zest

Preheat the oven to 350°F.

In a medium saucepan on low heat, warm the honey and sugar and add the butter to melt. Sift together ½ cup of the flour and the baking powder and baking soda into a bowl, and then stir into the warm honey mixture.

Add up to 1 cup of flour and the walnuts, orange zest, candied lemon and ginger, and spices to form a dough that is slightly sticky to the touch. Butter and flour an 8- × 8-inch pan, and line the bottom with parchment paper cut to fit. With moistened fingers press the mixture evenly into the pan.

Bake for 20 to 25 minutes.

Meanwhile, prepare the glaze. In a small saucepan on high heat, combine the sugar, honey, and lemon zest. Bring to a boil, and then remove from the heat.

While the bars are still warm, cut into rectangles or squares of desired size and brush with the glaze.

DARK CHOCOLATE
HONEY TRUFFLES

These truffles, which are dipped in chocolate, can be finished several ways. Right after dipping, roll them in sifted cocoa powder, grated chocolate, or ground toasted nuts. Or just dip them in cocoa powder *instead* of in melted chocolate.

MAKES ABOUT 4 DOZEN TRUFFLES

12 oz semisweet or bittersweet
  chocolate, plus 6 oz for dipping
1 cup honey

½ cup heavy cream (35%)
2 Tbsp unsalted butter

Chop 12 ounces of chocolate into small pieces and set aside.

In a medium saucepan, heat the honey and cream on medium to slightly below a simmer. Remove from the heat and add the chocolate. Stir until melted and smooth. Add the butter and stir until smooth. Refrigerate until completely chilled and firm.

To shape the truffles, take a spoonful of the mixture and roll into a ball about 1 inch in diameter. Place the rolled truffle onto a tray and continue with the rest of the mixture. Chill the truffles before finishing.

Chop the remaining 6 ounces of chocolate and place in a small heatproof bowl. Bring a small saucepan of water to a simmer and remove from the heat. Place the bowl over (but not touching) the hot water, and stir until the chocolate is melted and smooth. Take the bowl off the saucepan, and stir until the chocolate cools to body temperature.

With a fork, dip the truffles one at a time into the chocolate, shaking off the excess, and place on a parchment paper–lined or plastic-wrapped tray in a cool spot to firm up.

ALMOND NOUGAT (TORRONE)

For me, *torrone* always brings back memories of Christmas. These little sweet nougats, made with toasted nuts and citrus and covered in edible wafer paper, came in small matchbox-sized packages decorated with pictures of famous sites in Italy, such as the Leaning Tower of Pisa and the Roman Coliseum. It was always a special Christmas treat to receive them. Alba is a city in Piedmont, a northern province of Italy; the city and its surrounding area are famous for their hazelnuts, which are used in the torrone and many of the other sweets produced there. I do prefer almonds in torrone, but feel free to use the traditional hazelnuts, or even walnuts or pistachios, instead.

MAKES ONE 8- × 8-INCH PAN

Edible wafer paper (see Chef's Tip)

1 lb slivered blanched almonds

½ cup less 1 Tbsp granulated sugar

¼ cup water

1¼ cups honey

1 large egg white

1 Tbsp grated orange zest
 (and/or lemon zest)

Preheat the oven to 350°F.

Line the bottom and sides of an 8- × 8-inch pan with parchment paper cut to fit, and then line the bottom with edible wafer paper cut to fit. Set aside.

Place the almonds on a baking sheet and toast for 10 minutes. Turn off the oven, and keep the almonds warm in the oven while preparing the rest of the ingredients.

In a medium heavy-bottomed saucepan on medium heat, bring the sugar and water to a boil. Add the honey and cook until a candy thermometer reads 290°F. Turn the heat to the lowest setting to keep the mixture warm.

Beat the egg white using an electric mixer or stand mixer until firm peaks form. With your mixer still running, carefully pour the hot syrup down the side of the bowl into the egg white. Turn the speed down to medium.

Add the toasted almonds and orange zest and continue to beat on medium speed for 5 minutes to cool slightly. Pour the mixture into the prepared pan, and top with another layer of wafer paper.

Lay a flat board or another pan on top of the nougat, and then top with a weight of at least 2 pounds.

When cooled but still slightly soft, about 40 minutes, remove the weight and the board or pan. Tip the torrone onto a clean cutting board. Coat a chef's knife with nonstick cooking spray or wipe it with an oiled cloth, and cut the torrone into desired shapes. Let cool completely. Store in an airtight container. The pieces can also be individually wrapped in parchment or decorative foil to make a unique gift.

CHEF'S TIP

Wafer paper, although difficult to find, adds authenticity to the recipe. It's usually made from potato or rice starch. If you can't find it, liberally dust the parchment paper lining the bottom of the pan as well as the top of the torrone with sifted icing sugar.

SAUCES, SPREADS, AND PRESERVES

FIG BARBECUE SAUCE

Near the end of summer, there's always an abundance of fresh local fruit, whether at farmers' markets or supermarkets or in your own backyard. Figs are my favorite fruit, and I was inspired to make a barbecue sauce with them. Figs contain a lot of natural sugar, and their flavor combines very well with honey.

MAKES ABOUT 3 CUPS, ENOUGH FOR AT LEAST 4 SLABS OF PORK RIBS

12 oz fresh ripe figs (8–10 figs)

⅔ cup chopped yellow onion

4 large cloves garlic, chopped

⅓ cup balsamic vinegar

⅓ cup (2½ fl oz) red wine

1 tsp red chili flakes or to taste

1 tsp ground cloves

⅓ cup honey

Salt and freshly ground black pepper, to taste

Combine all of the ingredients in a heavy-bottomed saucepan, and bring to a simmer on low heat. Cook for 1 hour. Cool slightly and purée the mixture using a blender or food processor. If you desire a smoother sauce, press through a fine-meshed sieve.

This sauce will keep for several weeks in the refrigerator.

FIG AND BALSAMIC SPREAD

Try this spread on crackers or toasted bread with rich creamy cheeses such as mascarpone, Brie, or Camembert; they're a great match with the slight tartness of the spread. (Try using other tart fruits such as grapes and plums.) Top with a slice of fresh fig or whatever fruit is in season. The texture can be adjusted to personal preference. For a firm spread, just reduce the mixture a little more; for something smoother, pulse the figs in a food processor.

MAKES 1½–1¾ CUPS

10 oz fresh figs (6–8 figs)

2 Tbsp balsamic vinegar

¼ tsp (or a good pinch) ground cloves

¼ tsp (or a good pinch) table salt

¼ cup honey

Trim off the stem ends of the figs, and coarsely chop. Place the figs in a heavy-bottomed pot or saucepan, and add the vinegar, cloves, and salt. Bring to a boil. Turn down the heat to low and reduce the mixture to a thick paste, stirring often to prevent sticking. This can take up to 20 minutes. Be patient and avoid the urge to increase the heat—that may cause the mixture to scorch due to the high sugar content of the figs.

Stir in the honey. Transfer to a clean container; you can do this while still warm. Let it cool to room temperature, and then cover and refrigerate for up to 3 weeks.

 Bees communicate through chemical scents called pheromones and through special dances.

NASTURTIUM BUTTER

This is something a little different to spread on crusty rolls or bread. It also works well as a last-minute touch for steamed or grilled fish—it bastes and flavors at the same time. Omit the salt and pepper and increase the honey, and you have an interesting topping for your morning toast. For an even more colorful butter, combine several different varieties of edible petals.

MAKES TWO 5 OZ ROLLS

½ lb (1 cup) unsalted butter, softened

1 cup washed and dried fresh
   nasturtium flowers

1 Tbsp green nasturtium seeds,
   crushed and minced

½–1 Tbsp honey

⅛ tsp freshly ground black pepper

⅛ tsp table salt (optional)

Place all of the ingredients in a bowl, and blend using a wooden spoon or spatula until thoroughly combined.

Lay out an 8- × 10-inch piece of plastic wrap or waxed paper. Spoon half of the butter onto it, and roll into a tight cylinder. Lay out another piece of plastic wrap or waxed paper, and repeat with the rest of the butter. Chill until firm, and slice off the butter as needed. (The finished rolls of butter also freeze very well. Thaw in the refrigerator before using.)

Alternatively, spoon the entire mixture into a covered container and refrigerate.

 It takes nectar from around 2 million flowers to make 1 pound (½ kg) of honey.

RASPBERRY HONEY SYRUP

The most appreciated gifts are sometimes the most simple. A bottle of Raspberry Honey Syrup in your next Christmas basket will go over very well. It's delicious as a substitute for maple syrup or as something to drizzle over ice cream—anytime you'd like a little flavor of summer.

MAKES ABOUT 7 CUPS

2 lb fresh or frozen raspberries
   (about 6 cups)
1½ cups water
4 lb (5 cups) honey

EQUIPMENT

Glass bottles or canning jars for 7 cups
   of syrup

Sterilize the bottles or jars by placing them in a large pot. Cover with water and bring to a simmer. Keep submerged and hot.

Combine the raspberries and water in a pot and bring to a simmer on medium heat. Cook for 20 minutes or until the berries have broken down. Avoid stirring too much or pressing on the berries. This will help keep the syrup clear.

Strain the mixture through several layers of cheesecloth or a jelly bag into a clean pot. Discard the raspberries. Add the honey to the syrup and stir to combine. Heat the mixture to 180°F.

Carefully remove the bottles or jars from the hot water. Transfer the syrup to the hot bottles/jars, leaving no more than ½ inch of space below the rim, and screw on the caps. Set aside to cool undisturbed.

Store in a cool dark place, and store any opened bottles in the refrigerator.

WILD BERRY HONEY VINEGAR

This uniquely flavored vinegar adds a distinct edge to salad dressing, even when used in small amounts. I like to flavor rich savory sauces for red game meat, such as venison, with a little bit of this vinegar. Use a combination of seasonal berries or do separate batches with each kind. Some of the more unusual berries I've used are salal berries and Oregon grapes.

MAKES ABOUT 6 CUPS

1 lb berries (about 3 cups)

4 cups white wine vinegar

1 lb (1¼ cups) honey

EQUIPMENT

Glass bottles for 6 cups of vinegar

Combine the berries and vinegar in a nonreactive pot and heat to 180°F. Pour into a glass or enamel pot and let cool. Cover and let sit undisturbed in a cool room for 2 weeks.

Strain through several layers of cheesecloth without pressing.

Sterilize the bottles by placing them in a large pot. Cover with water and bring to a simmer. Keep submerged and hot.

Place the vinegar again in a nonreactive pot, and stir in the honey. Heat to 180°F. Carefully remove the bottles from the hot water. Using a funnel, pour the vinegar into the hot bottles and cap.

CHEF'S TIP

Nonreactive pots such as stainless steel or enamel-coated are preferable to aluminum, copper, and cast iron, which may react with the acid in the vinegar and produce undesirable flavors.

HONEY LEMON JELLY

A wonderful topping for your toast in the morning, this jelly also works well for flavoring whipped cream or to add a little zip to a savory sauce for chicken or fish.

MAKES 4 HALF-PINT (1-CUP) JARS

2 Tbsp grated lemon zest

¾ cup fresh lemon juice, strained
   to remove the seeds

2½ cups honey

1 (3 fl oz) pouch liquid pectin

EQUIPMENT

4 half-pint (1-cup) canning jars

Canning pot

Place the jars into the canning pot, cover with water, and bring to a simmer. Keep submerged and hot. In a separate small pan, add the lids and screw bands and bring to a simmer (but do not boil). Keep submerged and hot on low heat.

Combine the lemon zest, lemon juice, and honey in a medium saucepan and stir well. Bring to a rolling boil on high heat, stirring constantly. Add the pectin and boil for 1 minute. Remove from the heat and skim off any foam.

Carefully remove the jars from the hot water. Pour the jelly into the hot jars, filling to within ¼ inch of the rims.

Wipe the rims with a clean wet cloth, and then top with the lids and screw on the bands fingertip tight (do not overtighten). Place the jars on a rack in the canning pot, making sure the jars are covered by at least 1 inch of water.

Process the jars in a boiling water bath for 5 minutes. Remove from the canning pot and cool, undisturbed, on a wire rack.

HONEY APPLE JAM

A delicious spread as it is, this recipe also works well with the addition of 1/2 cup of walnut pieces or raisins. Just add at the same time as the lemon zest.

MAKES FOUR 1-PINT (2-CUP) JARS

3 lb tart apples (such as Granny Smith)
 or full-flavored, underripe apples,
 peeled and diced (8 cups)
1⅓ cups fresh lemon juice, divided
½ (2 oz) package Certo pectin crystals
2 cups granulated sugar

1⅓ cups honey
2 Tbsp grated lemon zest

EQUIPMENT
Four 1-pint (2-cup) canning jars
Canning pot

Place the jars into the canning pot, cover with water, and bring to a simmer. Keep submerged and hot. In a separate small pan, add the lids and screw bands and bring to a simmer (but do not boil). Keep submerged and hot on low heat.

Combine the apples and half of the lemon juice in a heavy-bottomed pot, and bring to a boil on high heat. Cook for 5 minutes or until the fruit begins to break up into a chunky sauce.

Dissolve the pectin in the remaining lemon juice, and stir into the apple mixture. Bring to a boil, add the sugar and honey, and boil on high heat for 1 minute. Stir in the lemon zest.

Remove from the heat and stir for 5 minutes, skimming off and discarding any foam that may have risen to the top.

Carefully remove the jars from the hot water. Fill the hot jars to within ¼ inch of the rims.

Wipe the rims with a clean wet cloth, and then top with the lids and screw on the bands fingertip tight (do not overtighten). Place the jars on a rack in the canning pot, making sure the jars are covered by at least 1 inch of water.

Process the jars for 10 minutes. Remove from the canning pot and cool, undisturbed, on a wire rack.

SOUR-CHERRY
MUSTARD PRESERVES

Sour cherries can be a little difficult to find, but they are definitely worth seeking out. The best source would be farmers' markets when the cherries are in season, usually in July, or perhaps a local retailer could special-order them for you. These wonderful preserves make a unique accompaniment for all types of roasted meats.

MAKES 4 HALF-PINT (1-CUP) JARS

2 lb sour cherries (about 6 cups)

2 cups berry sugar

1¾ cups honey

Juice of 2 lemons

2 Tbsp whole-grain Dijon mustard

2 tsp unsalted butter

EQUIPMENT

4 half-pint (1-cup) canning jars

Canning pot

Wash and gently dry the cherries. Pit them and combine with the sugar and honey. Allow the mixture to sit, covered, in a cool spot for 24 hours.

The next day, place the jars into the canning pot, cover with water, and bring to a simmer. Keep submerged and hot. In a separate small pan, add the lids and screw bands and bring to a simmer (but do not boil). Keep submerged and hot on low heat.

In a large heavy-bottomed saucepan, combine the cherries with the lemon juice, mustard, and butter, and bring to a rapid boil on high heat. Boil for 4 minutes. Skim off any foam that rises to the top. The mixture should be thickened with little juice remaining.

Carefully remove the jars from the hot water. Fill the hot jars with the preserves to within ¼ inch of the rims. Wipe the rims with a clean wet cloth, and then top with the lids and screw on the bands fingertip tight (do not overtighten). Place the jars on a rack in the canning pot, making sure the jars are covered by at least 1 inch of water.

Process the jars for 20 minutes. Remove from the canning pot and cool, undisturbed, on a wire rack.

APPLE AND GREEN
GRAPE BUTTER

This is a good use for those grapes that don't ripen during a cooler fall. The simple flavors of the fruit really come through. Add ½ teaspoon each of ground cinnamon, ginger, and cloves for a more autumnal flavor. For best results use a cooking apple, such as McIntosh, Braeburn, Winesap, or Jonagold.

MAKES 4 CUPS

1½ cups green seedless grapes (½ lb)

1½ cups chopped unpeeled apples
  (2 large apples)

1 Tbsp grated lemon zest

1 Tbsp fresh lemon juice

¼ cup water

⅔ cup granulated sugar

½ cup honey

EQUIPMENT

Canning jars for 4 cups of apple and
  grape butter

Canning pot

Place the jars into the canning pot, cover with water, and bring to a simmer. Keep submerged and hot. In a separate small pan, add the lids and screw bands and bring to a simmer (but do not boil). Keep submerged and hot on low heat.

Combine the grapes, apples, lemon zest, lemon juice, and water in a heavy-bottomed pot. Bring to a simmer on medium heat and cook until the grapes and apples are soft, about 10 to 15 minutes.

Press the mixture through a fine-meshed sieve or a food mill. This will remove the skins and seeds. Return the purée to the pot, and add the sugar.

Bring the mixture to a boil on high heat. Reduce the heat to medium and simmer, stirring often, until the mixture has reduced to a thick paste, about 15 to 20 minutes. Stir in the honey, bring to a simmer, and reduce again to a thick paste.

To test whether the butter is done, place a small amount on a plate. When no liquid separates from the edge of the apple and grape butter, it is done.

Carefully remove the jars from the hot water. Pour the apple and grape butter into the hot jars. Wipe the rims with a clean wet cloth, and then top with the lids and screw on the bands. Let cool, and store in the refrigerator.

 Bees have strawlike tongues called *proboscises*, which they use to suck up liquids. They also have mandibles so they can chew.

HONEY PEACHES

Use firm, slightly underripe peaches here. It will be harder to overcook them and they will maintain their shape.

MAKES SIX 1-PINT (2-CUP) JARS

¼ cup fresh lemon juice

5½ lb peaches

1¼ cups honey

6 small strips lemon zest

3 vanilla beans, cut in half and
   split open (optional)

EQUIPMENT

Six 1-pint (2-cup) canning jars

Canning pot

Place the jars into the canning pot, cover with water, and bring to a simmer. Keep submerged and hot. In a separate small pan, add the lids and screw bands and bring to a simmer (but do not boil). Keep submerged and hot on low heat.

In a large bowl, combine the lemon juice and ¼ cup water and set aside. Peel, pit, and cut the peaches into wedges, dropping the wedges into the lemon water as they are cut, making sure they get coated completely.

Bring the honey and 2½ cups water to a simmer in a saucepan to create a syrup for the peaches. Cover the saucepan to keep hot on low heat.

Carefully remove the jars from the hot water. Remove the peach wedges from the lemon water, and carefully pack them into the hot jars. Fill the jars with the honey syrup to within ¼ inch of the rims. Place a strip of lemon zest and one half-piece of vanilla bean in each jar.

Wipe the rims with a clean wet cloth, and then top with the lids and screw on the bands fingertip tight (do not overtighten). Place the jars on a rack in the canning pot, making sure the jars are covered by at least 1 inch of water.

Bring to a rolling boil and process for 25 minutes. Remove the jars carefully from the canning pot and cool, undisturbed, on a wire rack.

SPICED CARROTS

You can easily substitute parsnips for the carrots. Pickling spice can be purchased ready to use. It's a mixture of spices that includes mustard and coriander seeds, allspice berries, whole cloves, red chili flakes, and bay leaves. Any additions to the spice mix are up to the individual cook; feel free to add any of the "sweet" spices, as I like to call them, such as cinnamon and nutmeg.

MAKES SIX 1-PINT (2-CUP) JARS

3 lb baby carrots or peeled carrots

4 cups white vinegar

2½ cups honey

3 Tbsp pickling spice (see headnote)

1 Tbsp pickling salt

EQUIPMENT

Six 1-pint (2-cup) canning jars

Canning pot

Cut the carrots into ½-inch rounds, or into sticks about 1 inch shorter than the height of the jars.

Place the jars into the canning pot, cover with water, and bring to a simmer. Keep submerged and hot. In a separate small pan, add the lids and screw bands and bring to a simmer (but do not boil). Keep submerged and hot on low heat.

In a small saucepan, combine the vinegar, honey, pickling spice, and pickling salt. Bring to a boil on high heat, remove from the heat, and cover to keep warm.

Carefully remove the jars from the hot water. Pack the carrots into the hot jars, and fill with the pickling liquid to within ¼ inch of the rims.

Wipe the rims with a clean wet cloth, and then top with the lids and screw on the bands fingertip tight (do not overtighten). Place the jars on a rack in the canning pot, making sure the jars are covered by at least 1 inch of water.

Bring to a boil and process for 30 minutes. Remove the jars from the canning pot carefully and cool, undisturbed, on a wire rack.

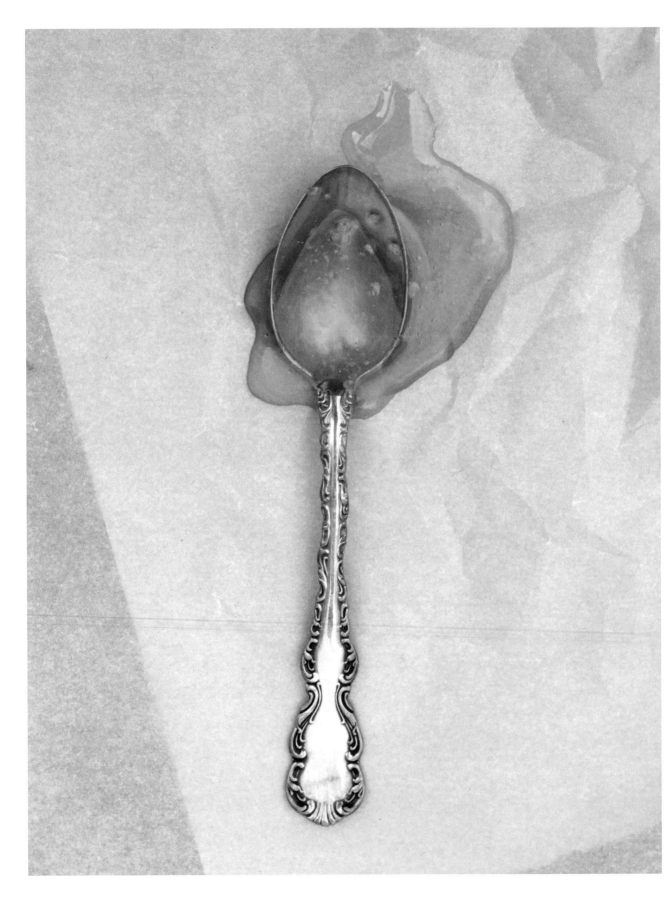

BEVERAGES

GINGER LEMON SODA

This makes a very refreshing hot-weather drink. Make the base recipe and store it in the fridge, and top with soda whenever you feel thirsty! I usually multiply this recipe. If you have Limoncello (Italian lemon liqueur), add 2 tablespoons (1 fluid ounce) to each glass before topping with the soda. If you have mint in your garden, bruise some freshly picked mint and add it to the drink.

SERVES 4

¼ cup grated fresh ginger

1 medium lemon, thinly sliced,
   plus more for serving

1 cup boiling water

⅓ cup honey

Ice cubes

3 cups soda water

Place the ginger and lemon slices in a heatproof bowl. Pour the boiling water over the mixture and set aside to steep for 15 minutes.

Strain the mixture through a sieve into a tall pitcher, and stir in the honey. Add ice cubes and top with the soda water. Garnish with extra lemon slices.

CHEF'S TIP
Do not oversteep the lemon slices; the peel may make this drink bitter.

BANANA AND YOGURT
PEANUT-BUTTER SMOOTHIE

Of course you can substitute any nut butter for the peanut butter.

MAKES ABOUT 3 CUPS; SERVES 4

2 ripe bananas

½ cup low-fat yogurt

½–1 cup orange juice, more if needed

¼ cup smooth organic peanut butter

2 Tbsp honey or to taste

Combine all of the ingredients in a blender and blend until smooth. Thin to desired consistency with extra orange juice.

APRICOT HONEY LIQUEUR

I've enjoyed making my own liqueurs since I was young (and legal). They are very easy to make and are a great way to preserve a little bit of summer, especially when using your own homegrown fruit. For an aperitif, pour 2 tablespoons (1 fluid ounce) over ice, and top with sparkling water or sparkling wine. Or serve on its own as an after-dinner liqueur with dessert.

MAKES 1 QUART (4 CUPS)

12 fresh organic apricots

3 cups (24 fl oz) brandy

6 whole cloves

Zest of 1 lemon, cut into thin strips

1½ cups honey

Split the apricots in half, remove the pits, and cut into quarters. Place into a large jar and add the brandy, cloves, and lemon zest. Cover tightly and set aside in a cool dark spot for 1 month.

Strain through several layers of cheesecloth, discarding the fruit. Stir in the honey. Rinse the jar and add the mixture back into the jar. Cover tightly and set aside in a cool dark spot undisturbed for 2 more weeks.

Carefully strain again through several layers of cheesecloth, being careful to leave behind any sediment that may be at the bottom of the jar.

CHEF'S TIP

This liqueur will keep indefinitely. There may be some sediment in the bottom of the jar; if it bothers you, strain the liqueur through a coffee filter a few times.

APPLE BRANDY LIQUEUR

Choose apples that are slightly sweet, such as McIntosh or Red Delicious, and fully ripe. This liqueur will keep indefinitely. You may see some sediment at the bottom of the jar; if it bothers you, strain the liqueur through a coffee filter a few times.

MAKES 1 QUART (4 CUPS)

4 cups peeled and chopped apples (1½ lb)	3 whole allspice
	Zest of 1 lemon, cut into strips
2 cinnamon sticks	3 cups brandy
3 whole cloves	1¼ cups buckwheat honey

Combine all of the ingredients except the honey in a very large jar with a tight-fitting lid. Set aside in a cool dark spot for 1 month.

Strain the liquid through several layers of cheesecloth into a clean bowl. (Leave the apples and spices in the cheesecloth; do not discard.) Stir in the honey until dissolved. Strain again through a coffee filter into a clean 1-quart (4-cup) container.

Form a bundle with the cheesecloth, and hang from a kitchen cabinet or other spot over a bowl. Let drip for several hours or overnight without squeezing or pressing. Strain the extra liquid through a coffee filter and add to the rest of the liqueur.

Set aside in a cool dark spot for 1 month to allow any residual sediment to settle. Serve as an after-dinner drink with fruit desserts.

CHEF'S TIP

When you're done straining the excess brandy from the apples and spices, discard the spices. Purée the apple pieces to add to your favorite quick-bread recipe.

MEXICAN HOT CHOCOLATE WITH HONEY AND CHIPOTLE

We've been drinking hot chocolate for thousands of years. Our versions today are much richer than what they used to drink in the past. The original recipe was ground cocoa beans, water, wine, and hot peppers. When the Spaniards discovered the drink, they started sweetening it with sugar. Whatever the history, this spicy hot chocolate is a delicious treat and a great way to send a little surprise to your guests.

MAKES 6 GENEROUS MUGS

8 oz semisweet or bittersweet
   chocolate

5 cups whole milk

½ cup heavy cream (35%)

3 Tbsp honey or to taste

¼ tsp ground cinnamon

1 whole dried chipotle pepper

Chop the chocolate into roughly ½-inch pieces and set aside. In a heavy-bottomed pot, combine the milk, cream, honey, cinnamon, and chipotle. Heat on medium and bring to a simmer.

Add the chocolate all at once, and whisk constantly until the chocolate is completely melted. Taste and remove the chipotle pepper once you have the desired spice level.

Whisk vigorously to foam the hot chocolate and pour into 6 large mugs.

HONEY ESPRESSO THREE WAYS

This is several recipes in one. The first is a hot spiced espresso sweetened, of course, with honey. The mixture can also be cooled and combined with either soda water or milk for a refreshing summer drink.

MAKES 4 BEVERAGES

1 cup freshly brewed espresso

¼ cup honey

A good pinch of ground ginger

A good pinch of ground cinnamon

Combine all of the ingredients in a large glass measuring cup, and divide into 4 espresso cups. If desired, top with a spoonful of honey-flavored whipped cream.

To make a cold beverage, cool the mixture in the refrigerator. Divide into four 10-ounce glasses filled with ice cubes. Fill to the top with soda water or milk.

METRIC CONVERSION CHARTS

VOLUME	
⅛ tsp	0.5 mL
¼ tsp	1 mL
½ tsp	2.5 mL
¾ tsp	4 mL
1 tsp	5 mL
1½ tsp	7.5 mL
2 tsp	10 mL
1 Tbsp	15 mL
4 tsp	20 mL
2 Tbsp	30 mL
3 Tbsp	45 mL
¼ cup/4 Tbsp	60 mL
5 Tbsp	75 mL
⅓ cup	80 mL
½ cup	125 mL
⅔ cup	160 mL
¾ cup	185 mL

1 cup	250 mL
1¼ cups	310 mL
1½ cups	375 mL
1¾ cups	435 mL
2 cups/1 pint	500 mL
2¼ cups	560 mL
2½ cups	625 mL
3 cups	750 mL
3½ cups	875 mL
4 cups/1 quart	1 L
4½ cups	1.125 L
5 cups	1.25 L
5½ cups	1.375 L
6 cups	1.5 L
6½ cups	1.625 L
7 cups	1.75 L
8 cups	2 L

½ fl oz	15 mL
1 fl oz	30 mL
1½ fl oz	45 mL
2 fl oz	60 mL
2½ fl oz	80 mL
3 fl oz	90 mL
4 fl oz	125 mL
5 fl oz	160 mL
6 fl oz	185 mL
8 fl oz	250 mL
24 fl oz	750 mL

WEIGHT	
1 oz	30 g
2 oz	60 g
3 oz	90 g
¼ lb/4 oz	125 g
5 oz	150 g
6 oz	175 g
½ lb/8 oz	250 g
9 oz	270 g
10 oz	300 g
¾ lb/12 oz	375 g
14 oz	400 g
1 lb	500 g
1½ lb	750 g
2 lb	1 kg
2½ lb	1.25 kg
3 lb	1.5 kg
4 lb	1.8 kg
5 lb	2.3 kg
5½ lb	2.5 kg
6 lb	2.7 kg

LENGTH	
⅛ inch	3 mm
¼ inch	6 mm
⅜ inch	9 mm
½ inch	1.25 cm
¾ inch	2 cm
1 inch	2.5 cm
1½ inches	4 cm
2 inches	5 cm
3 inches	8 cm
4 inches	10 cm
4½ inches	11 cm
5 inches	12 cm
6 inches	15 cm
7 inches	18 cm
8 inches	20 cm
8½ inches	22 cm
9 inches	23 cm
10 inches	25 cm
11 inches	28 cm
12 inches	30 cm

OVEN TEMPERATURE	
140°F	60°C
145°F	63°C
250°F	120°C
275°F	140°C
300°F	150°C
325°F	160°C
350°F	180°C
375°F	190°C
400°F	200°C
425°F	220°C
450°F	230°C
475°F	240°C
500°F	260°C

DEEP-FRYING AND CANDY-MAKING TEMPERATURE	
160°F	71°C
220°F	104°C
265°F	129°C
290°F	143°C
360°F	182°C
370°F	188°C
375°F	191°C

INDEX

TouchWood Editions
touchwoodeditions.com

LIBRARY AND ARCHIVES CANADA CATALOGUING IN PUBLICATION
Prosperi-Porta, Angelo, author
Honey : everyday recipes for cooking and baking with
nature's sweetest secret ingredient / Angelo Prosperi-Porta.

Includes index.
Issued in print and electronic formats.
ISBN 978-1-77151-108-7

1. Cooking (Honey). 2. Cookbooks. I. Title.

TX767.H7P76 2015   641.6'8   C2014-908207-X

Editor: Grace Yaginuma
Proofreader: Cailey Cavallin
Design: Pete Kohut
Food photography: Nadine Boyd
except on pages viii, 54, 57, 107, 108, 120, 140 by Gary Faessler

Canadian   Patrimoine
Heritage   canadien

We gratefully acknowledge the financial support for our publishing activities from
the Canada Book Fund and the British Columbia Book Publishing Tax Credit.

This book was produced using FSC®-certified, acid-free papers,
processed chlorine free, and printed with vegetable-based inks.

The information in this book is true and complete to the best of the author's knowledge.
All recommendations are made without guarantee on the part of the author.
The author disclaims any liability in connection with the use of this information.

1 2 3 4 5   19 18 17 16 15

PRINTED IN CANADA